# Campbell

# CREATIVE COOKING
# WITH SOUP

| | |
|---|---|
| Cooking with Soup... Your Way | 2 |
| How to Use This Book | 3 |
| Appetizers | 4 |
| Soups | 14 |
| Main Dishes | 26 |
| Accompaniments | 58 |
| Salads and Dressings | 68 |
| Sauces | 76 |
| Soup Surprises | 84 |
| Index | 94 |

# Cooking with Soup... Your Way

Did you ever wish someone would write a cookbook just for you? Someone has, and it's different from any other cookbook you've ever used. That's because it's planned for flexibility—to help you with your busy schedule, your family's tastes, your budget, your food supplies, even your creativity.

Each recipe includes a unique chart that shows you how to vary ingredients to suit your needs. For example, if a recipe suggests peas and you don't like peas, you can use another alternative—possibly corn or spinach. If you're all out of cream of mushroom soup, the recipe might suggest using cream of celery. Or, if your budget favors tuna over shrimp, you can take that option.

Today's Americans are becoming more and more interested in the quality and nutrition of the foods they eat. They are learning that good food habits are essential to health and a general feeling of well-being. We at Campbell are excited about this trend. We believe that good food contributes greatly to the quality of life.

One of the easiest ways to balance your diet is to eat a wide variety of foods. Each single food has something important to contribute to your health, but it takes a combination of foods to complete the nutritional balance.

That's how this book fits into your plan for good eating. With the wide choice of ingredients in each recipe chart, you can easily vary your diet according to your nutritional needs and tastes.

These variations make every recipe a springboard to as many as 256 different dishes, for a total of more than 8,000 combinations in the book. The secret to making these recipes so versatile is the magic of canned soup. Cream-style soups start a foolproof sauce for dishes that require one; broth-based soups add a blend of seasonings to foods cooked with liquid.

If you're a beginning cook, you'll appreciate the simplicity of recipes made with soup. If you're more experienced, you'll enjoy the versatility of using soup to create your own new recipes.

You're already familiar with soup as a good old-fashioned food, but soup is also very contemporary. It goes into pasta and pizza, quiche and kabobs, tacos and stir-frys, even vegetarian main dishes. Besides these tempting entrées are fresh salads, full-flavored appetizers, hearty soups, even delicious desserts.

You can use these recipes with confidence because they have been carefully tested in Campbell's kitchens. Each variation has been created to work well with every other ingredient combination on the chart. Once you start using the recipes, you'll find your own favorites and you'll see how well they fit into your busy lifestyle. Yes, this book really is written for you!

# How to Use This Book

Each recipe in this book consists of three parts: an ingredient list, a chart and preparation instructions.

## Souper Easy Quiche

Ingredient List

4 eggs
1 can (10¾ to 11 ounces) condensed **Soup**
½ cup light cream
1 cup shredded **Cheese**
**Meat**
½ cup **Vegetable**
1 9-inch unbaked piecrust
Ground nutmeg

### Chart

| Soup | Cheese | Meat | Vegetable |
|------|--------|------|-----------|
| Cheddar cheese | sharp Cheddar | ½ cup diced cooked ham | drained, cooked chopped broccoli |
| cream of mushroom | American | 6 slices bacon, cooked, drained and crumbled | drained, cooked cut asparagus |
| cream of onion | Monterey Jack | ½ cup diced cooked chicken | sliced mushrooms |
| cream of celery | Swiss | ½ cup diced cooked turkey | drained, cooked chopped spinach |

### Preparation Instructions

1. In medium bowl, beat eggs until foamy. Gradually add **Soup** and cream, mixing well.

2. Sprinkle **Cheese, Meat** and **Vegetable** evenly over piecrust. Pour soup mixture over all. Sprinkle with nutmeg.

3. Bake at 350°F. 50 minutes or until center is set. Let stand 10 minutes before serving. Makes 6 servings.

Simply read the ingredient list as you would a normal recipe. When you come to an ingredient in **bold** type, refer to the chart. Choose from one of the options listed below the heading. For example, for 1 can condensed **Soup**, look under the heading "Soup" and choose from Cheddar cheese soup, cream of mushroom, cream of onion and cream of celery.

There are 2 ways to use this chart. You may choose all the items from a single horizontal row as indicated in red or you may skip around as indicated in green. Once you have made all your selections, just follow the numbered steps.

That's all there is to it! You'll be preparing new recipes in no time.

# *Appetizers*

⚜

# Appetizer Cheesecake

2 tablespoons butter or margarine
1 cup zwieback crumbs
1 can (10¾ to 11 ounces) condensed **Soup**
1 container (15 ounces) ricotta cheese
2 packages (8 ounces each) cream cheese, softened
**Cheese**
2 eggs
1 clove garlic, minced
**Seasoning**
1 cup sour cream
**Topper**

| Soup | Cheese | Seasoning | Topper |
|---|---|---|---|
| cream of celery | 1 cup grated Romano | ¼ teaspoon thyme leaves, crushed | caviar and sieved hard-cooked egg yolk |
| Cheddar cheese | 1½ cups shredded Cheddar | 3 tablespoons chopped fresh chives | sliced cucumber, green onion and fresh dill sprigs |
| tomato | 1½ cups shredded Swiss | ½ teaspoon basil leaves, crushed | tomato roses and green onion tops |
| cream of chicken | 1½ cups shredded Muenster | 1 teaspoon curry powder | chutney |

1. **In small saucepan over medium heat, melt butter; stir in crumbs. Press mixture firmly onto bottom of 9-inch springform pan.**

2. **In food processor or large bowl, combine Soup,** ricotta cheese and cream cheese. **Process with food processor or beat with electric mixer until smooth. Add Cheese, eggs, garlic and Seasoning.** Beat until smooth. Turn into prepared pan and place in jelly-roll pan.

3. **Bake at 325°F. 1½ hours or until puffy and lightly browned. Cool completely in pan on wire rack. Cover; refrigerate until serving time, at least 2 hours.**

4. **Spread sour cream over cake; garnish with Topper.** Makes 16 appetizer servings.

# Cheese Ball

1 can (11¼ to 11½ ounces) condensed **Soup**
¼ cup salsa
3 cups shredded **Cheese**
**Seasoning**
**Coating**
Assorted crackers

| Soup | Cheese | Seasoning | Coating |
|---|---|---|---|
| bean with bacon | sharp Cheddar | 1 clove garlic, minced | chopped fresh parsley |
| chili beef | Monterey Jack | ½ teaspoon hot pepper sauce | finely crushed corn chips |
| split pea with ham and bacon | American | ½ teaspoon dry mustard | chopped walnuts |

1. In medium bowl with mixer at low speed or in food processor, beat or process **Soup,** salsa, **Cheese** and **Seasoning** until as smooth as possible. Cover and chill 4 hours or overnight.

2. On waxed paper, place **Coating.** Shape cheese mixture into ball and roll in coating until well covered. Serve with crackers. Makes 1 ball, 16 appetizer servings.

# Avocado Dip

1 can (10½ to 10¾ ounces) condensed **Soup**
1 package (8 ounces) cream cheese, softened
**Seasoning 1**
**Seasoning 2**
1 ripe avocado, peeled and seeded
**Dipper**

| Soup | Seasoning 1 | Seasoning 2 | Dipper |
|---|---|---|---|
| cream of celery | 1 tablespoon finely chopped onion | 1 tablespoon chili powder | tortilla chips |
| cream of shrimp | 1 tablespoon finely chopped shallots | 2 teaspoons finely chopped, seeded jalapeño peppers | thinly sliced bagels, toasted |
| cream of chicken | 1 clove garlic, minced | ¼ teaspoon hot pepper sauce | assorted raw vegetables |

In medium bowl with mixer at low speed, gradually beat **Soup** into cream cheese until smooth. Beat in **Seasoning 1** and **Seasoning 2.** Mash avocado; beat into soup mixture. Serve with **Dipper.** Makes about 2 cups.

# Rumaki Spread

6 slices bacon
1 pound chicken livers
2 envelopes unflavored gelatin
**Liquid**
1 can (10¾ ounces) condensed **Soup**
¼ cup chopped water chestnuts
**Flavoring**
**Accompaniment**

| Liquid | Soup | Flavoring | Accompaniment |
|---|---|---|---|
| ¼ cup dry sherry plus ½ cup water | cream of onion | ¼ cup chopped green onions | party rye rounds |
| ¼ cup dry white wine plus ½ cup water | cream of celery | 2 hard-cooked eggs, chopped | melba toast |
| ¾ cup water | cream of mushroom | 2 tablespoons chopped fresh chives | wheat crackers |
| ¾ cup apple juice | cream of chicken | 1 teaspoon curry powder | sliced French bread |

1. In 10-inch skillet over medium heat, cook bacon until browned. Remove from skillet; drain on paper towels. Crumble and set aside.

2. Add chicken livers to pan drippings; cook until livers are tender, but still pink inside, stirring frequently. Remove from heat.

3. In small saucepan, sprinkle gelatin over **Liquid** to soften. Over low heat, heat until gelatin dissolves, stirring often. Remove from heat.

4. In food processor or blender container, combine **Soup,** cooked chicken livers and gelatin mixture. Process or blend until smooth. Pour into medium bowl. Stir in bacon, water chestnuts and **Flavoring.** Pour into 3-cup mold. Cover; refrigerate until set, at least 4 hours.

5. Unmold onto serving platter; serve with **Accompaniment.** Makes 16 appetizer servings.

# Cheese-Stuffed Vegetables

1 can (10½ to 10¾ ounces) condensed **Soup**
1 package (8 ounces) cream cheese, softened
1 to 2 tablespoons lemon juice
1 clove garlic, minced
½ teaspoon **Herb,** crushed
¼ teaspoon **Spice**
**Vegetables**
Chopped fresh parsley

| Soup | Herb | Spice | Vegetables |
|------|------|-------|------------|
| cream of onion | summer savory leaves | pepper | cherry tomatoes, tops and centers removed |
| cream of celery | tarragon leaves | ground nutmeg | celery stalks, cut into 2-inch pieces |
| cream of mushroom | thyme leaves | paprika | snow pea pods, cut open |

1. In medium bowl with mixer at low speed, beat **Soup** into cream cheese until well blended. Beat in lemon juice, garlic, **Herb** and **Spice.** Cover; refrigerate until serving time, at least 4 hours.

2. Using a spoon or decorating tube, stuff cheese mixture into **Vegetables.** Sprinkle with parsley. Makes about 2¼ cups filling, 36 appetizers.

**Tip:** *To prepare cherry tomatoes for stuffing, slice off the tops, then scoop out the seeds and pulp with a small spoon or grapefruit knife. With a sharp knife, cut a decorative edge, if desired. To prepare pea pods for stuffing, make a slit in one long edge with a sharp knife.*

# Mexican-Style Appetizer

1 can (11½ ounces) condensed bean with bacon soup
1 package (1¼ ounces) taco seasoning mix
¼ teaspoon hot pepper sauce
1 cup sour cream
1 can (4 ounces) chopped green chilies, drained
½ cup **Flavoring**
1 cup shredded **Cheese**
½ cup **Topper**
½ cup chopped tomato
**Dipper**

| Flavoring | Cheese | Topper | Dipper |
|-----------|--------|--------|--------|
| sliced pimento-stuffed olives | longhorn | alfalfa sprouts | tortilla chips |
| diced cooked ham | Monterey Jack | chopped green pepper | pita bread, torn and toasted |
| diced avocado | Cheddar | shredded lettuce | celery sticks |
| diced pepperoni | mozzarella | chopped celery with leaves | sliced jícama |

1. In small bowl, combine soup with taco seasoning mix and hot pepper sauce; stir until blended. On large serving plate, spread mixture into a 6-inch round. Spread sides and top of bean mixture with sour cream to cover.

2. Layer chilies, **Flavoring, Cheese, Topper** and tomato over sour cream. Cover; refrigerate until serving time, at least 4 hours. Surround with **Dipper**. Makes 10 appetizer servings.

**Tip:** *Jícama is a Mexican vegetable that is becoming more readily available in U.S. markets. It is shaped like a turnip, has a brown skin, and may be cooked or eaten raw. To prepare, simply peel jicama and cut into thin slices or strips.*

# Tomato Cheese Fondue

2 tablespoons butter or margarine
1 cup chopped tomatoes
½ cup chopped onion
1 clove garlic, minced
1 can (10¾ to 11 ounces) condensed **Soup**
**Seasoning**
**Cheese,** shredded
**Dipper**

| Soup | Seasoning | Cheese | Dipper |
|---|---|---|---|
| cream of mushroom | ½ teaspoon oregano leaves, crushed | 1½ pounds sharp Cheddar | French bread cubes |
| cream of onion | ½ teaspoon marjoram leaves, crushed | 1 pound natural Swiss | celery sticks |
| cream of celery | ⅛ teaspoon hot pepper sauce | 1½ pounds Gruyère | corn chips |
| Cheddar cheese | ¼ teaspoon dry mustard | 1½ pounds Monterey Jack | apple wedges |

1. In 3-quart saucepan over medium heat, in hot butter, cook tomatoes, onion and garlic 10 minutes or until mixture is slightly thickened, stirring often.

2. Stir in **Soup** and **Seasoning.** Gradually add **Cheese,** stirring until smooth after each addition.

3. Pour cheese mixture into fondue pot and keep warm. Serve with **Dipper.** Makes about 3½ cups.

*To Microwave:* In 2-quart microwave-safe casserole, combine butter, tomatoes, onion and garlic; cover. Microwave on HIGH 3 to 4 minutes until onion is tender, stirring once. Stir in **Soup, Seasoning** and **Cheese.** Microwave on HIGH 4 to 6 minutes until cheese melts, stirring occasionally. Proceed as in Step 3.

**Tip:** *If fondue becomes too thick, stir in a little milk.*

# French Pizza Slices

½ pound bulk pork sausage
½ cup chopped onion
1 clove garlic, minced
1 can (10¾ ounces) condensed tomato soup
**Vegetable**
½ teaspoon **Herb,** crushed
**Seasoning**
1 loaf (12 to 14 inches) French bread, halved lengthwise
1 cup shredded **Cheese**

| Vegetable | Herb | Seasoning | Cheese |
|---|---|---|---|
| ½ cup sliced mushrooms | oregano leaves | few drops hot pepper sauce | mozzarella |
| ½ cup chopped green pepper | basil leaves | 1 teaspoon chili powder | Cheddar |
| ½ cup sliced pitted ripe olives | marjoram leaves | 2 tablespoons grated Romano cheese | American |
| ¼ cup chopped green chilies | Italian seasoning | ½ teaspoon ground cumin | Monterey Jack |

1. In 10-inch skillet over medium heat, cook sausage, onion and garlic until vegetables are tender and sausage is well browned, stirring occasionally to break up meat. Pour off fat.

2. Add soup, **Vegetable, Herb** and **Seasoning.** Heat to boiling; reduce heat to low. Simmer, uncovered, 5 minutes. Remove from heat; cool slightly.

3. Arrange bread cut side up on baking sheet. Spoon soup mixture on bread; sprinkle with **Cheese.** Bake at 450°F. 15 minutes or until hot. Cut each bread half into 8 slices to serve. Makes 16 appetizers.

**Tip:** *To make ahead, prepare as above, but do not bake. Freeze until firm. When frozen, wrap in foil; return to freezer. Unwrap; place frozen bread on baking sheet. Bake at 450°F. 20 to 25 minutes until heated through.*

# *Soups*

## ✣

# Chili

1 pound **Meat**
1 cup chopped onion
~~1 cup chopped green pepper~~
2 cloves garlic, minced
2 cans (10½ to 10¾ ounces each) condensed **Soup**
1 can (about 15 ounces) **Vegetable**   *Corn + Kidney Beans*
1 ~~2~~ tablespoons chili powder
~~1 tablespoon vinegar~~   *2 TBS Steak Sauce*
**Garnish**

| Meat | Soup | Vegetable | Garnish |
|---|---|---|---|
| ground beef | tomato rice | kidney beans | shredded Cheddar cheese |
| bulk pork sausage | Spanish style vegetable | mixed vegetables | green pepper rings |
| Italian sausage, casings removed | tomato bisque | garbanzo beans | sour cream and sliced green onions |
| ground pork | tomato | whole kernel corn | crushed corn chips |

1. In 4-quart Dutch oven over medium heat, cook **Meat,** onion, green pepper and garlic until meat is browned and vegetables are tender, stirring occasionally to break up meat. Pour off fat.

2. Stir in **Soup, Vegetable** and its liquid, chili powder and vinegar. Heat to boiling. Reduce heat to low; simmer, uncovered, 30 minutes, stirring occasionally.

3. Ladle into bowls; top with **Garnish.** Makes about 6½ cups, 6 servings.

*To Microwave:* In 2-quart microwave-safe casserole, crumble **Meat.** Add onion, green pepper and garlic; cover. Microwave on HIGH 7 to 9 minutes until meat is nearly done, stirring occasionally. Pour off fat. Stir in **Soup, Vegetable** and its liquid, chili powder and vinegar; cover. Microwave on HIGH 12 to 15 minutes until heated through, stirring occasionally. Ladle into bowls; top with **Garnish.**

# Pasta and Bean Soup

**Meat**
½ cup chopped onion
½ cup chopped celery
½ cup shredded carrot
1 clove garlic, minced
1 can (10½ ounces) condensed **Soup**
1 soup can water
1 can (19 ounces) white kidney beans
½ teaspoon **Herb,** crushed
1 bay leaf
⅛ teaspoon pepper
½ cup uncooked **Pasta**

| Meat | Soup | Herb | Pasta |
|------|------|------|-------|
| ½ cup diced cooked ham plus 2 tablespoons salad oil | vegetable | thyme leaves | small shell macaroni |
| 4 slices bacon, diced | Spanish style vegetable | oregano leaves | ditalini |
| 4 ounces bulk pork sausage, crumbled | minestrone | basil leaves | elbow macaroni |

1. In 4-quart Dutch oven over medium heat, cook **Meat** until lightly browned, stirring occasionally. Add onion, celery, carrot and garlic; cook until vegetables are tender, stirring occasionally.

2. Stir in **Soup,** water, beans with their liquid, **Herb,** bay leaf and pepper. Heat to boiling. Reduce heat to low. Cover; simmer 15 minutes.

3. Stir in **Pasta;** cook about 12 minutes more or until pasta is tender. Discard bay leaf. Makes about 5 cups, 4 servings.

**Tip:** *Ditalini is a type of macaroni that is often included in Italian soups. It is shaped like short tubes.*

# Easy Pea Soup

1 cup diced potato
½ cup chopped onion
**Vegetable**
**Herb**
1 cup chicken broth
½ cup water
1 can (11¼ ounces) condensed green pea soup
½ cup **Liquid**
**Garnish**

| Vegetable | Herb | Liquid | Garnish |
|---|---|---|---|
| 1 cup carrots cut into julienne strips | ½ teaspoon summer savory leaves, crushed | half-and-half | sour cream |
| 1 cup sliced celery | 1 tablespoon chopped fresh parsley | milk | crumbled cooked bacon |
| 1 large tomato, chopped | ½ teaspoon oregano leaves, crushed | additional water | fresh mint leaves |
| 1 cup fresh or frozen peas | ¼ teaspoon rubbed sage | additional chicken broth | seasoned croutons |

1. In 2-quart saucepan over medium heat, heat potato, onion, **Vegetable, Herb,** chicken broth and water to boiling. Reduce heat to low. Cover; simmer 10 minutes or until vegetables are tender.

2. Meanwhile, in medium bowl, combine pea soup and **Liquid;** stir until smooth. Add to broth mixture. Heat through. Ladle into bowls; top with **Garnish.** Makes about 4 cups, 4 servings.

*To Microwave:* In 2-quart microwave-safe casserole, combine potato, onion, **Vegetable, Herb,** chicken broth and water; cover. Microwave on HIGH 8 to 10 minutes until vegetables are tender, stirring once. Meanwhile, in medium bowl, combine pea soup and **Liquid;** stir until smooth. Add to broth mixture; cover. Microwave on HIGH 4 to 6 minutes until heated through, stirring once. Ladle into bowls; top with **Garnish.**

**Tip:** *To make seasoned croutons, cut 2 slices bread into ½-inch cubes. In small skillet, melt 1 tablespoon butter or margarine; stir in bread cubes. Cook over medium heat until bread is browned, stirring often. Toss with 1 tablespoon grated Parmesan cheese.*

# Extra-Good Cream Soup

2 tablespoons butter or margarine
½ cup chopped onion
**Vegetable**
½ teaspoon **Herb,** crushed
1 can (10½ to 10¾ ounces) condensed **Soup**
½ cup light cream
¾ cup milk
**Garnish**

| Vegetable | Herb | Soup | Garnish |
|-----------|------|------|---------|
| 1 medium tomato, diced | tarragon leaves | tomato | grated Parmesan cheese |
| 1 cup sliced mushrooms | thyme leaves | cream of mushroom | chopped fresh parsley |
| 1 cup fresh or frozen cut asparagus | dill weed | cream of asparagus | oyster crackers |
| 1 cup sliced celery | marjoram leaves | cream of celery | melba toast |

1. In 2-quart saucepan over medium heat, in hot butter, cook onion, **Vegetable** and **Herb** until vegetables are tender, stirring occasionally.

2. Stir in **Soup,** cream and milk. Heat through, stirring occasionally. Ladle into bowls; serve with **Garnish.** Makes about 3½ cups, 4 servings.

*To Microwave:* In 2-quart microwave-safe casserole, combine butter, onion, **Vegetable** and **Herb;** cover. Microwave on HIGH 7 to 9 minutes until vegetables are tender, stirring once. Stir in **Soup,** cream and milk; cover. Microwave on HIGH 5 to 7 minutes until heated through, stirring occasionally. Ladle into bowls; serve with **Garnish.**

**Tip:** *Here's an extra-quick, extra-good chicken and corn soup: In medium saucepan, stir 1 can (10¾ ounces) condensed cream of chicken soup. Stir in 1 soup can milk, 1 can (5 ounces) chunk white chicken and 1 can (8 ounces) whole kernel corn. Heat to simmering, stirring often.*

# Speedy Potato Chowder

4 slices bacon, diced
½ cup chopped onion
1 can (10¾ ounces) condensed cream of potato soup
**Liquid**
1 can (about 8 ounces) **Vegetable**
**Meat**
2 tablespoons chopped fresh parsley

| Liquid | Vegetable | Meat |
|---|---|---|
| ¾ cup beer plus ¾ cup water | mixed vegetables | 1 cup sliced frankfurters |
| 1½ cups milk | whole kernel corn | 1 cup diced cooked chicken |
| 1 cup milk plus ½ cup light cream | lima beans | 1 cup diced cooked ham |
| 1 cup evaporated milk plus ½ cup water | diced carrots | 1 can (about 7 ounces) tuna, drained and flaked |

1. In 3-quart saucepan over medium heat, cook bacon until crisp. Remove with slotted spoon and drain on paper towels. Pour off all but 1 tablespoon bacon drippings.

2. In hot drippings, cook onion until tender, stirring occasionally. Stir in soup and **Liquid** until well mixed. Add **Vegetable** with its liquid, **Meat,** parsley and reserved bacon. Heat through, stirring occasionally. Makes about 4 cups, 4 servings.

*To Microwave:* In 2-quart microwave-safe casserole, place bacon; cover. Microwave on HIGH 3 to 4 minutes until crisp, stirring once. With slotted spoon, remove bacon; drain on paper towels. Pour off all but 1 tablespoon bacon drippings. To drippings, add onion; cover. Microwave on HIGH 2 to 2½ minutes until tender, stirring once. Stir in soup and **Liquid** until well mixed. Add **Vegetable** with its liquid, **Meat,** parsley and reserved bacon; cover. Microwave on HIGH 8 to 10 minutes until heated through, stirring occasionally.

**Tip:** *If you don't have leftover ham or chicken, buy it already cooked at your supermarket's delicatessen. You'll need about 5 ounces cooked chicken or ham to make 1 cup diced.*

# Skillet Seafood Bisque

¼ cup butter or margarine
1 cup sliced mushrooms
**Vegetable**
1 clove garlic, minced
3 tablespoons all-purpose flour
1 can (10¾ ounces) condensed chicken broth
**Seafood**
**Liquid**
1 tablespoon chopped fresh parsley
**Garnish**

| Vegetable | Seafood | Liquid | Garnish |
|-----------|---------|--------|---------|
| 2 tablespoons chopped fresh chives | 1 pound medium shrimp, shelled and deveined | ½ cup dry white wine plus ½ cup heavy cream | fresh dill sprigs |
| ¼ cup chopped onion | 1 pound bay scallops | 1 cup half-and-half | grated Parmesan cheese |
| ¼ cup chopped green onions | 1 pound monkfish or other firm fish fillets, cubed | 1 cup milk | ground nutmeg |
| ½ cup chopped green pepper | 1 pint shucked clams, drained and chopped | 1 cup clam juice | cooked, crumbled bacon |

1. In 10-inch skillet over medium heat, in hot butter, cook mushrooms, **Vegetable** and garlic until vegetables are tender, stirring occasionally. Stir in flour until smooth. Gradually stir in chicken broth. Heat to boiling, stirring constantly.

2. Add **Seafood.** Reduce heat to low. Cover; simmer about 5 minutes or until seafood is done. Stir in **Liquid** and parsley; heat through. Ladle into bowls; top with **Garnish.** Makes about 4½ cups, 6 servings.

*Tip: Here's a speedy seafood soup: In medium saucepan, stir 1 can (10¾ ounces) condensed cream of mushroom soup. Stir in 1 soup can milk and 1 can (6½ ounces) minced clams with their liquid. Heat to simmering, stirring often.*

# Fish Stew

¼ cup salad oil
1 cup chopped onion
1 cup **Vegetable 1**
3 cloves garlic, minced
2 cans (10½ to 10¾ ounces each) condensed **Soup**
1 soup can water
1 can (6 ounces) tomato paste
**Vegetable 2**
1 bay leaf
**Herb,** crushed
2 pounds haddock or other fish fillets, cut into 1½-inch pieces
½ pound medium shrimp, shelled and deveined
12 medium clams in shells or 1 can (6½ ounces) minced clams

| Vegetable 1 | Soup | Vegetable 2 | Herb |
|---|---|---|---|
| chopped green pepper | chicken broth | 1 can (16 ounces) tomatoes, cut up (do not drain) | 1 teaspoon basil leaves |
| chopped celery and celery leaves | chicken vegetable | 2 cups diced peeled potatoes | ½ teaspoon tarragon leaves |
| chopped zucchini | chicken gumbo | 2 cups cubed eggplant | ½ teaspoon oregano leaves |
| shredded carrot | chicken with rice | 2 cups fresh or frozen whole kernel corn | 1 teaspoon dill weed |

1. In 5-quart Dutch oven over medium heat, in hot oil, cook onion, **Vegetable 1** and garlic until vegetables are tender, stirring occasionally.

2. Stir in **Soup,** water, tomato paste, **Vegetable 2,** bay leaf and **Herb.** Heat to boiling. Reduce heat; simmer, uncovered, 15 minutes.

3. Add fish, shrimp and clams. Cover; simmer 10 minutes or until fish flakes easily when tested with fork and clam shells are opened (discard any clams that do not open). Discard bay leaf. Makes about 10 cups, 8 servings.

# Soup Mates

One easy way to create a new soup is to combine two different condensed soups. Over the years, we have experimented with hundreds of combinations; here are some of our favorites.

To prepare soup mates, simply empty the soups into a saucepan. Gradually stir in the liquid; heat to simmer, stirring occasionally.

| Soup 1 | | Soup 2 | | Liquid |
|---|---|---|---|---|
| split pea with ham & bacon | + | cream of celery | + | 1 can milk plus 1 can water |
| golden mushroom | + | French onion | + | 1 can milk plus 1 can water |
| tomato | + | green pea | + | 1 can milk plus 1 can water |
| Cheddar cheese | + | cream of asparagus | + | 1 can milk plus 1 can water |
| chicken noodle | + | chicken & stars | + | 2 cans water |
| New England clam chowder | + | cream of mushroom | + | 1 can milk plus 1 can water |
| bean with bacon | + | tomato rice | + | 2 cans water |
| chicken gumbo | + | cream of celery | + | 1 can milk plus 1 can water |
| Cheddar cheese | + | tomato | + | 1 can milk plus 1 can water |
| chili beef | + | vegetable beef | + | 2 cans water |
| cream of chicken | + | green pea | + | 1 can milk plus 1 can water |
| black bean | + | golden mushroom | + | 2 cans water |
| tomato | + | beef noodle | + | 2 cans water |
| cream of celery | + | vegetarian vegetable | + | 1 can milk plus 1 can water |
| oyster stew | + | cream of potato | + | 2 cans milk |
| cream of mushroom | + | beef broth | + | 2 cans water |
| minestrone | + | Manhattan clam chowder | + | 2 cans water |
| turkey noodle | + | cream of celery | + | 1 can milk plus 1 can water |
| meatball alphabet | + | Cheddar cheese | + | 1 can milk plus 1 can water |
| cream of mushroom | + | tomato | + | 1 can milk plus 1 can water |
| bean with bacon | + | French onion | + | 2 cans water |
| chicken vegetable | + | cream of chicken | + | 1 can milk plus 1 can water |
| New England clam chowder | + | cream of asparagus | + | 2 cans milk |
| chicken gumbo | + | vegetable | + | 2 cans water |

# Main Dishes

❦

# Fruited Chops

2 tablespoons salad oil
1½ pounds **Chops,** each cut ½ inch thick
1 can (10¾ ounces) condensed chicken broth
2 tablespoons soy sauce
1 tablespoon vinegar
**Fruit**
2 tablespoons brown sugar
2 tablespoons cornstarch
1 teaspoon ground **Spice**
Hot cooked rice
**Garnish**

| Chops | Fruit | Spice | Garnish |
|---|---|---|---|
| pork | 1 large apple, cubed, plus ½ cup apple juice | ginger | sliced green onion |
| lamb | 4 orange slices, cut up, plus ½ cup orange juice | nutmeg | slivered orange peel |
| smoked pork | 1 can (8 ounces) pineapple slices, cut up | mace | chopped fresh parsley |
| veal | 1 can (8 ounces) apricot halves, cut up | cinnamon | sliced water chestnuts |

1. In 10-inch skillet over medium-high heat, in hot oil, cook **Chops** until browned on both sides.

2. Stir in chicken broth, soy sauce and vinegar. Heat to boiling; reduce heat to low. Cover; simmer 20 minutes or until chops are tender.

3. Meanwhile, drain **Fruit,** reserving liquid. Add enough water to liquid to make ½ cup, if necessary. In small bowl, combine liquid, brown sugar, cornstarch and **Spice;** stir until smooth.

4. Remove chops from skillet; keep warm. Stir cornstarch mixture into skillet. Over medium heat, heat to boiling. Add reserved fruit; heat through.

5. Arrange chops over rice; spoon sauce over chops. Top with **Garnish.** Makes 4 servings.

# Easy Pot Roast

**Fat**
3½-pound beef chuck pot roast
1 can (10¾ ounces) condensed **Soup**
**Herb**
2 tablespoons all-purpose flour
¼ cup **Liquid**

| Fat | Soup | Herb | Liquid |
|-----|------|------|--------|
| 2 tablespoons shortening | cream of onion | 1 teaspoon thyme leaves, crushed | water |
| 2 tablespoons salad oil | cream of mushroom | 1 teaspoon rosemary leaves, crushed | dry white wine |
| non-stick cooking spray | cream of celery | 1 teaspoon marjoram leaves, crushed | heavy cream |
| 2 tablespoons bacon drippings | golden mushroom | 1 bay leaf (remove before serving) | dry red wine |

1. In 6-quart Dutch oven over medium-high heat, in hot **Fat,** brown beef on all sides. Pour off fat.

2. Stir in **Soup** and **Herb.** Reduce heat to low. Cover; simmer 2½ to 3 hours until tender, stirring occasionally. Add water during cooking, if necessary.

3. Remove beef to platter; keep warm. In screw-top jar, shake together flour and **Liquid** until smooth; stir into pan drippings. Over high heat, heat to boiling, stirring constantly. Cook 1 minute more.

4. Cut meat into thin slices. Serve gravy with meat. Makes 8 servings.

**Tip:** *The cooking time needed for a pot roast depends on its shape as well as on its size. Thin roasts such as underblade roast need less time; blocky roasts such as shoulder roast need more.*

# Garden Swiss Steak

¼ cup all-purpose flour
1 pound beef round steak, cut ½ inch thick
2 tablespoons salad oil
1 clove garlic, minced
1 bay leaf
⅛ teaspoon pepper
1 can (10¾ ounces) condensed **Soup**
½ cup water
1 medium green pepper, cut into strips
**Vegetable 1**
½ cup **Vegetable 2**
**Accompaniment**

| Soup | Vegetable 1 | Vegetable 2 | Accompaniment |
|---|---|---|---|
| tomato | 1 medium onion, sliced | sliced mushrooms | hot mashed potatoes |
| cream of onion | 1 cup sliced zucchini | sliced carrots | hot buttered noodles |
| cream of mushroom | 6 green onions, sliced | chopped tomatoes | hot cooked rice |
| cream of potato | 1 cup sliced celery | sliced parsnips | hot biscuits |

1. On cutting board with meat mallet, pound flour into both sides of steak until all flour is absorbed and meat is slightly flattened. Cut steak into 4 serving-size pieces. In 10-inch skillet over medium-high heat, in hot oil, cook steak until browned on both sides.

2. Add garlic, bay leaf and pepper. Spoon **Soup** over meat; add water. Heat to boiling. Reduce heat to low. Cover; simmer 1 hour, stirring occasionally.

3. Add green pepper, **Vegetable 1** and **Vegetable 2.** Cover; simmer 30 minutes more or until meat is tender. Discard bay leaf. Serve with **Accompaniment.** Makes 4 servings.

**Tip:** *When using celery, chop a few celery leaves and add them to the skillet for extra flavor.*

# Stir-Fried Beef and Vegetables

½ pound boneless beef sirloin steak
1 can (10½ to 10¾ ounces) condensed **Soup**
1 tablespoon cornstarch
1 tablespoon soy sauce
3 tablespoons salad oil
1 clove garlic, minced
4 green onions, cut into 1-inch pieces
1 cup **Vegetable 1**
**Vegetable 2**
**Accompaniment**

| Soup | Vegetable 1 | Vegetable 2 | Accompaniment |
|---|---|---|---|
| beef broth | fresh or frozen cut broccoli | 1 can (8 ounces) sliced bamboo shoots, drained | shredded lettuce |
| French onion | sliced mushrooms | 1 cup diced tomatoes | hot cooked rice |
| chicken broth | fresh or frozen cut asparagus | 1 can (8 ounces) sliced water chestnuts, drained | hot cooked noodles |
| chicken with rice | sliced celery | 1 cup fresh or canned bean sprouts | chow mein noodles |

1. Freeze steak 1 hour to make slicing easier. Trim and discard excess fat from steak. Cut steak into very thin slices; set aside.

2. In small bowl, combine **Soup,** cornstarch and soy sauce; stir to blend. Set aside.

3. In 10-inch skillet or wok over medium-high heat, in 2 tablespoons hot oil, stir-fry beef strips and garlic until meat is browned; remove from skillet.

4. Add remaining 1 tablespoon oil to skillet. Add green onions and **Vegetable 1;** stir-fry 1 minute. Add **Vegetable 2;** stir-fry 30 seconds more.

5. Return beef to skillet. Stir soup mixture; stir into skillet. Heat to boiling; cook 1 minute more. Spoon over **Accompaniment.** Makes about 2½ cups, 2 servings.

**Tip:** *To make delicious sandwiches, spoon beef mixture into pita bread halves; omit* **Accompaniment.**

# Teriyaki Beef Kabobs

1 can (10½ to 11 ounces) condensed **Soup**
¼ cup dry sherry
¼ cup soy sauce
1 large clove garlic, minced
**Seasoning**
1 tablespoon **Sweetener**
1½ pounds boneless beef sirloin steak, cut 1 inch thick
1 medium green pepper, cut into 1-inch squares
1 pound small whole onions, cooked and drained
½ cup pineapple chunks
**Accompaniment**

| Soup | Seasoning | Sweetener | Accompaniment |
|---|---|---|---|
| Spanish style vegetable | ¼ cup sliced green onions | honey | hot cooked rice |
| French onion | ¼ cup finely chopped onion | brown sugar | hot cooked wild rice |
| beef broth | ½ teaspoon ground ginger | sugar | hot cooked bulgur wheat |
| tomato bisque | 1 teaspoon dry mustard | molasses | hot cooked noodles |

1. For marinade, in medium bowl, combine **Soup,** sherry, soy sauce, garlic, **Seasoning** and **Sweetener.**

2. Cut beef into 1-inch cubes; add to marinade. Cover; refrigerate 3 hours or overnight, turning once or twice.

3. Drain meat, reserving marinade. Thread beef cubes, green pepper, onions and pineapple chunks on six 12-inch skewers.

4. On rack in broiler pan, broil 6 inches from heat 10 minutes or until meat is cooked to desired doneness, turning and brushing often with marinade. Serve with **Accompaniment.** Makes 6 servings.

**Tip:** *Assemble skewers before marinating. Place in shallow dish; pour marinade over skewers. Cover; refrigerate 3 hours or overnight, turning occasionally.*

# Best-Ever Meat Loaf

1 can (10¾ to 11 ounces) condensed **Soup**
**Meat**
**Crumbs**
1 egg, beaten
⅓ cup finely chopped onion
**Seasoning**
⅓ cup water

| Soup | Meat | Crumbs | Seasoning |
|------|------|--------|-----------|
| golden mushroom | 2 pounds ground beef | ½ cup fine dry bread crumbs | 1 tablespoon Worcestershire |
| cream of mushroom | 2 pounds meat loaf mix (beef, pork, veal) | ½ cup quick-cooking oats | 1 tablespoon soy sauce |
| Cheddar cheese | 1½ pounds ground beef plus ½ pound Italian sausage, casings removed | ½ cup finely crushed saltines | ¼ cup chopped pimento-stuffed olives |

1. In large bowl, thoroughly mix ½ cup of the **Soup, Meat, Crumbs,** egg, onion and **Seasoning.** In 12 by 8-inch baking pan, firmly shape meat into 8 by 4-inch loaf.

2. Bake at 350°F. 1¼ hours or until done. Remove meat loaf to platter; keep warm.

3. Pour off all but 3 tablespoons drippings from pan. Stir remaining **Soup** and water into drippings in pan, scraping up brown bits from bottom. Over medium heat, heat soup mixture until hot, stirring constantly. Serve gravy with meat loaf. Makes 8 servings.

**Tip:** *If you use a glass baking dish for your meat loaf, prepare as above in steps 1 and 2. Pour 3 tablespoons drippings into a small saucepan; discard remaining drippings. Stir remaining* **Soup** *and water into saucepan. Over medium heat, heat soup mixture until hot, stirring constantly. Serve as above.*

# Stuffed Cabbage Leaves

1 pound **Meat**
½ cup chopped onion
1 can (10½ ounces) condensed beef broth
½ cup **Grain**
½ teaspoon grated lemon peel
½ cup **Fruit**
¼ cup chopped walnuts
¼ cup chopped fresh parsley
½ teaspoon dried mint leaves (optional)
1 medium head cabbage
1 can (10½ to 11 ounces) condensed **Soup**
¼ teaspoon ground cinnamon

| Meat | Grain | Fruit | Soup |
|------|-------|-------|------|
| ground pork | raw bulgur wheat | chopped apple | tomato plus 1 tablespoon lemon juice |
| ground lamb | raw brown rice | golden raisins | Spanish style vegetable |
| ground beef | raw regular rice | chopped dried apricots | tomato rice plus 1 tablespoon lemon juice |

1. In 10-inch skillet over medium heat, cook **Meat** and onion until meat is well browned, stirring occasionally to break up meat. Pour off fat.

2. Add beef broth, **Grain** and lemon peel. Heat to boiling. Reduce heat to low. Cover; simmer until grain is tender, about 45 minutes for brown rice or 20 to 25 minutes for regular rice or bulgur; add a little water during cooking if mixture becomes dry. Remove from heat. Stir in **Fruit,** walnuts, parsley and mint.

3. Meanwhile, in 4-quart saucepan over high heat, heat about 6 cups water to boiling. Add whole head of cabbage to boiling water. Reduce heat to low. Cover; simmer 1 to 2 minutes or until outer leaves are softened. Remove cabbage from water. Carefully remove 6 outer leaves. Reserve remaining cabbage for another use.

4. Drain cabbage leaves on paper towels. Lay leaves flat on cutting board and cut out any tough stems. Spoon about ¾ cup meat filling into center of one leaf. Fold in sides, then roll up from stem end to form a bundle. Repeat with remaining leaves and filling.

5. In medium bowl, stir together **Soup** and cinnamon. Pour ½ of the soup mixture into 12 by 8-inch baking dish. Place cabbage rolls seam side down in prepared dish. Pour remaining soup mixture over all. Cover with foil. Bake at 350°F. 35 minutes or until heated through. Makes 6 servings.

# Tacos

**Meat**
½ cup chopped onion
2 cloves garlic, minced
1 tablespoon chili powder
1 can (10½ to 11 ounces) condensed **Soup**
8 taco shells
1 cup shredded **Cheese**
Shredded lettuce
1 cup **Addition**

| Meat | Soup | Cheese | Addition |
|---|---|---|---|
| 1 pound ground beef | tomato | Cheddar | chopped tomatoes |
| 1 pound ground pork | tomato rice | longhorn | diced avocado |
| 1½ cups chopped cooked beef plus 2 tablespoons salad oil | Spanish style vegetable | Monterey Jack | chopped green onions |
| 1 pound bulk pork sausage | tomato bisque | American | salsa |

1. Preheat oven to 350°F. In 10-inch skillet over medium heat, cook **Meat,** onion, garlic and chili powder until meat is well browned, stirring to break up meat. Pour off fat. Stir in **Soup.** Heat through, stirring occasionally.

2. Place about ¼ cup meat mixture in each taco shell. Place on baking sheet. Bake 5 minutes. Top with **Cheese,** lettuce and **Addition.** Makes 8 tacos, 4 servings.

*To Microwave:* In 1½-quart microwave-safe casserole, crumble **Meat.** Add onion, garlic and chili powder; cover. Microwave on HIGH 6 to 8 minutes until meat is nearly done, stirring occasionally. Pour off fat. Stir in **Soup;** cover. Microwave on HIGH 2 to 3 minutes until heated through, stirring once. Place about ¼ cup meat mixture in each taco shell. In 12 by 8-inch microwave-safe dish, arrange taco shells. Microwave on HIGH 2 to 3 minutes. Top with **Cheese,** lettuce and **Addition.**

# Souper Enchiladas

½ cup salad oil
8 corn tortillas (6-inch)
1 cup chopped onion
1 large clove garlic, minced
1 can (11 to 11½ ounces) condensed **Soup**
2 cups shredded cooked **Meat**
½ cup water
1 teaspoon ground cumin
**Seasoning**
1 jar (8 ounces) taco sauce
1 cup shredded **Cheese**

| Soup | Meat | Seasoning | Cheese |
|------|------|-----------|--------|
| black bean | chicken | 1 can (4 ounces) chopped green chilies, drained | Cheddar |
| bean with bacon | pork | 2 jalapeño peppers, seeded and chopped | longhorn |
| chili beef | beef | ¼ teaspoon hot pepper sauce | Monterey Jack |

1. In 8-inch skillet over medium heat, in hot oil, fry tortillas, one at a time, 2 to 3 seconds on each side. Drain tortillas on paper towels.

2. Spoon about 2 tablespoons of the hot oil into 10-inch skillet. Over medium heat, in the 2 tablespoons oil, cook onion and garlic until tender, stirring occasionally. Stir in **Soup, Meat,** water, cumin and **Seasoning.** Heat through.

3. Spoon about ⅓ cup soup mixture onto each tortilla; roll up. Arrange filled tortillas in 12 by 8-inch baking dish. Pour taco sauce evenly over enchiladas. Sprinkle with **Cheese.** Cover with foil.

4. Bake at 350°F. 25 minutes. Uncover; bake 5 minutes more. Makes 4 servings.

*To Microwave:* Use ingredients as above but use only 1 tablespoon oil. In 2-quart microwave-safe casserole, combine only 1 tablespoon oil, onion and garlic; cover. Microwave on HIGH 2 to 3 minutes until tender. Stir in **Soup, Meat,** water, cumin and **Seasoning;** cover. Microwave on HIGH 4 to 6 minutes until heated through, stirring once. Let stand, covered. Meanwhile, wrap tortillas in paper towel and place in microwave oven. Microwave on HIGH 2 minutes or until tortillas are pliable. Assemble as in Step 3, placing filled tortillas in 12 by 8-inch microwave-safe dish. Pour taco sauce evenly over enchiladas; cover. Microwave on HIGH 8 to 10 minutes until hot, rotating dish once. Sprinkle with **Cheese.** Microwave on HIGH 2 to 3 minutes until cheese is melted.

# Meatball Stew

1 pound ground beef
**Crumbs**
½ teaspoon **Herb,** crushed
1 egg
1 clove garlic, minced
2 tablespoons salad oil
1 can (10½ to 11 ounces) condensed **Soup**
¼ cup water
3 medium potatoes, peeled and quartered
**Vegetable**
1 medium onion, cut into thin wedges
1 tablespoon chopped fresh parsley

| Crumbs | Herb | Soup | Vegetable |
|---|---|---|---|
| ½ cup soft bread crumbs | summer savory leaves | French onion | 3 medium carrots, cut into 1-inch chunks |
| ¼ cup seasoned fine dry bread crumbs | basil leaves | tomato bisque | 1½ cups celery cut into ½-inch chunks |
| ¼ cup finely crushed saltines | oregano leaves | vegetable beef | 1½ cups cut green beans |
| ¼ cup quick-cooking oats | thyme leaves | Spanish style vegetable | 3 medium parsnips, peeled and cut into 1-inch chunks |

1. In medium bowl, combine ground beef, **Crumbs, Herb,** egg and garlic; mix thoroughly. Shape into 20 meatballs.

2. In 10-inch skillet over medium heat, in hot oil, cook meatballs until browned on all sides. Pour off fat.

3. Stir **Soup** and water into skillet; stir in potatoes, **Vegetable** and onion. Heat to boiling. Reduce heat to low. Cover; simmer 30 minutes or until vegetables are tender, adding more water if needed. Garnish with parsley. Makes 4 servings.

**Tip:** *Don't overmix meat mixture or meat will become tough.*

# Chicken Paprika

2 tablespoons salad oil
2 pounds chicken parts
1 can (10¾ ounces) condensed **Soup**
**Vegetable**
1 medium onion, sliced and separated into rings
1 clove garlic, minced
2 teaspoons paprika
½ cup sour cream
**Accompaniment**

| Soup | Vegetable | Accompaniment |
|---|---|---|
| cream of chicken | 1 cup quartered mushrooms | hot cooked noodles |
| cream of onion | ½ cup diced celery | hot cooked rice |
| cream of mushroom | 1 cup chopped tomatoes | hot cooked wild rice |
| cream of celery | ½ cup diced carrots | hot cooked kasha |

1. In 10-inch skillet over medium heat, in hot oil, cook chicken until browned on all sides. Pour off fat. Stir in **Soup, Vegetable,** onion, garlic and paprika. Heat to boiling. Reduce heat to low. Cover; simmer 30 to 40 minutes until chicken is fork-tender.

2. Remove chicken to platter; keep warm. Stir sour cream into sauce; over low heat, heat through, stirring constantly. Spoon some of sauce over chicken. Serve chicken with **Accompaniment;** pass remaining sauce. Makes 4 servings.

**Tip:** *Kasha is a coarsely ground grain, usually buckwheat, that is prominent in Eastern European cuisines. Look for it near the rice or in the gourmet section of your supermarket.*

# Chicken Breasts in Mushroom Sauce

3 whole chicken breasts, skinned, boned and split
⅓ cup all-purpose flour
2 tablespoons salad oil
2 tablespoons butter or margarine
1 clove garlic, halved
1 cup sliced mushrooms
**Vegetable**
1 can (10½ to 10¾ ounces) condensed **Soup**
¼ cup **Wine**
Dash pepper
**Accompaniment**

| Vegetable | Soup | Wine | Accompaniment |
|---|---|---|---|
| ¼ cup sliced green onions | chicken gumbo | dry vermouth | hot cooked rice |
| ½ cup sliced celery | chicken with rice | dry sherry | hot mashed potatoes |
| ½ cup shredded carrot | chicken broth | dry white wine | hot cooked noodles |
| ¼ cup sliced leek | chicken vegetable | dry red wine | hot cooked bulgur wheat |

1. With meat mallet, pound chicken to ¼-inch thickness. Coat with flour.

2. In 10-inch skillet over medium heat, in hot oil and butter, cook garlic 30 seconds; discard garlic.

3. Cook chicken cutlets, 2 or 3 at a time, until lightly browned on both sides; remove from skillet. Repeat with remaining cutlets.

4. Add mushrooms and **Vegetable** to skillet; cook until vegetables are tender, stirring occasionally. Stir in **Soup, Wine** and pepper, scraping bottom to loosen brown bits. Return cutlets to skillet. Reduce heat to low. Cover; simmer 15 minutes or until chicken is fork-tender. Serve cutlets with sauce and **Accompaniment.** Makes 6 servings.

**Tip:** *Bulgur is precooked cracked wheat that is most often found in health food stores or Middle Eastern food shops. If you have a choice, purchase the coarse grind for use with this recipe.*

# Baked Chicken Florida

1 can (10½ to 10¾ ounces) condensed **Soup**
**Juice**
**Seasoning**
¼ teaspoon tarragon leaves, crushed
3 pounds chicken parts
1 tablespoon cornstarch
**Garnish**

| Soup | Juice | Seasoning | Garnish |
|------|-------|-----------|---------|
| Spanish style vegetable | ½ cup orange juice | ½ teaspoon minced fresh ginger root | orange wedges |
| chicken broth | ¼ cup lemon juice plus ¼ cup water | 1 clove garlic, minced | avocado slices |
| chicken with rice | ¼ cup lime juice plus ¼ cup water | 2 tablespoons chopped fresh chives | kiwi fruit slices |

1. For marinade, in small bowl, combine **Soup, Juice, Seasoning** and tarragon. In shallow baking dish, pour marinade over chicken. Cover; refrigerate at least 2 hours, turning chicken occasionally. Drain chicken, reserving marinade.

2. In shallow roasting pan, arrange chicken. Bake at 375°F. 50 minutes or until chicken is fork-tender, basting chicken frequently with marinade. Remove to serving platter; keep warm.

3. Pour remaining marinade and pan drippings into 1-quart saucepan; stir in cornstarch. Over medium heat, heat to boiling, stirring occasionally; cook 1 minute more. Spoon some sauce over chicken; pass remainder. Arrange **Garnish** around chicken. Makes 6 servings.

**Tip:** *A garnish of kiwi fruit can turn an ordinary dish into a picture-pretty one. To use kiwi, simply peel the brown skin with a vegetable peeler or paring knife, then cut the fruit into slices.*

# Supper à la King

¼ cup butter or margarine
½ cup diced green pepper
⅓ cup chopped onion
1 can (10¾ ounces) condensed **Soup**
¾ cup milk
2 cups cubed cooked **Meat**
¾ cup shredded **Cheese**
¼ cup diced pimento
**Accompaniment**

| Soup | Meat | Cheese | Accompaniment |
|------|------|--------|---------------|
| cream of chicken | chicken | Swiss | shredded zucchini, cooked and drained |
| cream of asparagus | ham | Cheddar | baked potatoes, split |
| cream of mushroom | turkey | Muenster | cooked spaghetti squash (see **Tip** below) |
| cream of celery | kielbasa | American | biscuits, split |

1. In 10-inch skillet over medium heat, in hot butter, cook green pepper and onion until tender, stirring occasionally. Stir in **Soup** and milk; blend well. Stir in **Meat, Cheese** and pimento. Cook 5 minutes more or until heated through.

2. Arrange **Accompaniment** on serving platter. Serve sauce over accompaniment. Makes about 3½ cups sauce, 6 servings.

*To Microwave:* Use ingredients as above but use only 2 tablespoons butter. In 2-quart microwave-safe casserole, combine only 2 tablespoons butter, green pepper and onion; cover. Microwave on HIGH 2 to 3 minutes until vegetables are tender. Stir in **Soup** and milk; blend well. Stir in **Meat, Cheese** and pimento; cover. Microwave on HIGH 7 to 9 minutes until heated through, stirring occasionally. Serve as above.

**Tip:** *To cook spaghetti squash: Halve squash lengthwise; remove seeds and stringy portions. In 10-inch skillet, place squash halves cut side up. Add 1 inch water. Over medium heat, heat to boiling. Reduce heat to low. Cover; simmer 30 minutes or until fork-tender. Drain. With fork, scrape spaghetti-like strands from squash shell; place on serving platter. Discard shells.*

# Chicken-Stuffing Bake

1 cup water
¼ cup butter or margarine
1 package (7 ounces) seasoned stuffing mix
1 can (10¾ to 11 ounces) condensed **Soup**
½ cup mayonnaise
⅓ cup milk
2 cups diced cooked chicken or turkey
2 stalks celery, chopped
1 cup drained, cooked **Vegetable**
½ teaspoon **Seasoning**
**Cheese**

| Soup | Vegetable | Seasoning | Cheese |
|------|-----------|-----------|--------|
| cream of chicken | peas | thyme leaves, crushed | 1 cup shredded Cheddar |
| cream of mushroom | mixed vegetables | marjoram leaves, crushed | 1 cup shredded Swiss |
| cream of onion | chopped spinach | rubbed sage | 1 cup shredded Monterey Jack |
| Cheddar cheese | chopped broccoli | poultry seasoning | ¼ cup grated Parmesan |

1. In 1-quart saucepan over high heat, heat water and butter to boiling. In large bowl, pour hot water mixture over stuffing mix; toss to mix well. Pat ½ of the stuffing mixture into 12 by 8-inch baking dish.

2. In medium bowl, stir together **Soup,** mayonnaise, milk, chicken, celery, **Vegetable** and **Seasoning** until well mixed. Spoon evenly over stuffing mixture in baking dish; top with remaining stuffing mixture.

3. Bake at 400°F. 30 minutes or until heated through. Sprinkle with **Cheese.** Bake 5 minutes more or until cheese is melted. Makes 6 servings.

*To Microwave:* Prepare as in Steps 1 and 2 but assemble in 12 by 8-inch microwave-safe dish; cover. Microwave on HIGH 8 to 10 minutes until heated through, rotating dish once. Sprinkle with **Cheese.** Microwave on HIGH 2 minutes or until cheese is melted.

# Vegetable Lasagna

2 tablespoons olive or salad oil
1 large onion, chopped
1 clove garlic, minced
1 teaspoon Italian seasoning, crushed
**Vegetable**
1 can (10¾ to 11 ounces) condensed **Soup**
**Cheese**
1 egg
1 jar (32 ounces) spaghetti sauce
**Liquid**
9 lasagna noodles, cooked and drained
2 cups shredded mozzarella cheese

| Vegetable | Soup | Cheese | Liquid |
|---|---|---|---|
| 2 packages (10 ounces each) frozen chopped broccoli, thawed and drained | cream of chicken | 2 cups shredded sharp Cheddar | ½ cup dry red wine |
| 2 packages (10 ounces each) frozen chopped spinach, thawed and drained | cream of mushroom | 1 cup grated Parmesan | 1 cup heavy cream |
| 4 cups sliced zucchini | cream of celery | 2 cups shredded Swiss | 2 tablespoons vinegar plus ½ cup water |
| 2 packages (9 ounces each) frozen cut green beans, thawed and drained | Cheddar cheese | 1 cup ricotta plus ¼ cup crumbled blue cheese | ½ cup plain yogurt |

1. In 10-inch skillet over medium heat, in hot oil, cook onion, garlic and Italian seasoning until onion is tender, stirring occasionally. Stir in **Vegetable;** cook until vegetable is tender and liquid evaporates. Remove from heat; stir in **Soup, Cheese** and egg. Set filling aside.

2. In medium bowl, stir together spaghetti sauce and **Liquid;** pour ½ of the sauce mixture into 13 by 9-inch baking dish. Set remainder aside.

3. Arrange 3 lasagna noodles over sauce; spread with ½ of the vegetable filling. Sprinkle with ⅓ of the mozzarella. Arrange 3 more noodles over cheese; spread with remaining filling. Sprinkle with another ⅓ of the mozzarella. Top with remaining 3 noodles and remaining sauce.

4. Bake at 350°F. 40 minutes or until hot. Sprinkle with remaining ⅓ of the mozzarella; bake 5 minutes more. Let stand 15 minutes before serving. Makes 6 servings.

# Vegetable-Stuffed Fish Rolls

½ cup chopped tomato
½ cup chopped mushrooms
¼ cup chopped green onions
1 can (10¾ to 11 ounces) condensed **Soup**
6 **Fish** fillets (1½ pounds)
¼ cup **Liquid**
1 cup shredded **Cheese**

| Soup | Fish | Liquid | Cheese |
|------|------|--------|--------|
| cream of shrimp | flounder | dry sherry | Swiss |
| cream of mushroom | sole | dry white wine | Provolone |
| Cheddar cheese | perch | milk | sharp Cheddar |
| cream of celery | haddock | water | Muenster |

1. In medium bowl, combine tomato, mushrooms, green onions and ¼ cup of the **Soup.** Place about 3 tablespoons of the mixture on each **Fish** fillet and roll up. Secure with toothpicks if needed. Place fish rolls seam side down in 10 by 6-inch baking dish. Bake at 350°F. 25 minutes or until fish flakes easily when tested with fork. Discard any liquid in baking dish.

2. Meanwhile, in 2-quart saucepan, combine remaining **Soup** and **Liquid.** Over medium heat, heat through. Pour sauce over fish rolls; sprinkle with **Cheese.**

3. Bake 2 minutes more or until cheese is melted. Makes 6 servings.

***To Microwave:*** In medium bowl, combine tomato, mushrooms, green onions and ¼ cup of the **Soup.** Fill and roll **Fish** as directed. Place fish rolls seam side down in 10 by 6-inch microwave-safe dish; cover. Microwave on HIGH 8 to 14 minutes until fish flakes easily when tested with fork, rotating dish twice. Discard any liquid in dish. Let stand, covered, 2 to 3 minutes. Meanwhile, in 2-cup glass measure, combine remaining **Soup** and **Liquid.** Microwave on HIGH 2 minutes or until hot. Pour sauce over fish rolls; top with **Cheese.** Microwave on HIGH 1 minute more or until cheese is melted.

# Perfect Tuna Casserole

1 can (10¾ ounces) condensed **Soup**
¼ cup milk
1 can (about 7 ounces) tuna, drained and flaked
2 hard-cooked eggs, sliced
1 cup drained, cooked **Vegetable**
**Topper**

| Soup | Vegetable | Topper |
| --- | --- | --- |
| cream of mushroom | peas | ½ cup coarsely crumbled potato chips |
| cream of onion | cut green beans | 3 slices American cheese, cut into slivers |
| cream of shrimp | cut broccoli | ¼ cup toasted sliced almonds |
| New England clam chowder | whole kernel corn | 1 medium tomato, sliced |

1. In 1-quart casserole, stir together **Soup** and milk until well mixed. Stir in tuna, eggs and **Vegetable.**

2. Bake at 350°F. 25 minutes or until hot; stir.

3. Garnish with **Topper;** bake 5 minutes more. Makes 4 servings.

*To Microwave:* In 1-quart microwave-safe casserole, stir together **Soup** and milk. Stir in tuna, eggs and **Vegetable;** cover. Microwave on HIGH 8 to 10 minutes until hot, stirring occasionally. Garnish with **Topper.** Microwave on HIGH 1 to 3 minutes more until heated through.

**Tip:** *Toast almonds while the casserole is cooking in step 2. Simply spread almonds in a shallow baking pan and bake alongside the casserole 5 to 10 minutes until almonds are golden, stirring once or twice.*

# Pasta with White Seafood Sauce

½ cup butter or margarine
½ cup salad or olive oil
4 cloves garlic, minced
1 can (10¾ ounces) condensed chicken broth
**Herb**
**Seafood**
12 ounces **Pasta,** cooked and drained
Grated Parmesan or Romano cheese

| Herb | Seafood | Pasta |
|---|---|---|
| ¼ cup chopped fresh parsley | 1 can (6½ ounces) chopped clams | spaghetti |
| ½ cup chopped fresh basil | 1 can (6½ ounces) tuna packed in water | linguine |
| ¼ cup chopped fresh chives | 1 can (7 ounces) salmon | corkscrew macaroni |
| 1 teaspoon oregano leaves, crushed | 1 can (4½ ounces) shrimp, drained | medium noodles |

1. In 3-quart saucepan over medium heat, in hot butter and oil, cook garlic until golden. Add broth and **Herb.** Heat to boiling; reduce heat to low. Simmer, uncovered, 10 minutes.

2. Add **Seafood** with its liquid (do not use shrimp liquid); simmer 2 minutes more, stirring gently to break up tuna or salmon. Serve sauce over hot cooked **Pasta.** Pass grated cheese. Makes 6 servings.

**Tip:** *It's easy to chop fresh herbs such as parsley, basil and chives with kitchen shears. For parsley and basil, place the leaves in a cup or on a cutting board and use the shears to cut them into small pieces. For chives, simply snip short lengths right off the plant.*

# Souper Easy Quiche

4 eggs
1 can (10¾ to 11 ounces) condensed **Soup**
½ cup light cream
1 cup shredded **Cheese**
**Meat**
½ cup **Vegetable**
1 9-inch unbaked piecrust
Ground nutmeg

| Soup | Cheese | Meat | Vegetable |
|------|--------|------|-----------|
| Cheddar cheese | sharp Cheddar | ½ cup diced cooked ham | drained, cooked chopped broccoli |
| cream of mushroom | American | 6 slices bacon, cooked, drained and crumbled | drained, cooked cut asparagus |
| cream of onion | Monterey Jack | ½ cup diced cooked chicken | sliced mushrooms |
| cream of celery | Swiss | ½ cup diced cooked turkey | drained, cooked chopped spinach |

1. In medium bowl, beat eggs until foamy. Gradually add **Soup** and cream, mixing well.

2. Sprinkle **Cheese, Meat** and **Vegetable** evenly over piecrust. Pour soup mixture over all. Sprinkle with nutmeg.

3. Bake at 350°F. 50 minutes or until center is set. Let stand 10 minutes before serving. Makes 6 servings.

**Tip:** *To make piecrust: In medium bowl, stir together 1 cup all-purpose flour and ½ teaspoon salt. With pastry blender, cut in ⅓ cup shortening until mixture resembles coarse crumbs. Add 2 to 3 tablespoons cold water, a tablespoon at a time, mixing lightly with fork until pastry holds together. Form into a ball. On lightly floured surface, roll dough to a 13-inch round. Transfer to 9-inch pie plate. Trim edge, leaving ½ inch pastry beyond edge of pie plate. Fold overhang under pastry; pinch a high edge. Flute edge.*

# Easy Soufflé

1 can (10½ to 11 ounces) condensed **Soup**
1 cup shredded **Cheese**
**Seasoning**
6 eggs, separated

| Soup | Cheese | Seasoning |
|---|---|---|
| Cheddar cheese | sharp Cheddar | dash cayenne pepper |
| cream of asparagus | Swiss | ⅛ teaspoon ground nutmeg |
| tomato | American | ¼ teaspoon marjoram leaves, crushed |
| cream of chicken | Jarlsberg | 2 tablespoons chopped fresh parsley |

1. In 1-quart saucepan, combine **Soup, Cheese** and **Seasoning.** Over low heat, heat until cheese melts, stirring occasionally. Remove from heat.

2. In large bowl with mixer at high speed, beat egg whites until stiff peaks form; set aside. In small bowl with mixer at high speed, beat egg yolks until thick and lemon-colored. Gradually stir in soup mixture; fold into egg whites.

3. Pour into ungreased 2-quart casserole or soufflé dish. Bake at 300°F. 1 hour or until soufflé is lightly browned. Serve immediately. Makes 6 servings.

**Tip:** *For best results when beating egg whites, bring them to room temperature before you begin beating. Be sure to use a very clean bowl and beaters; even a small amount of fat or yolk will inhibit the beating.*

# *Accompaniments*

❦

# Vegetables Oriental

1 can (10½ to 10¾ ounces) condensed **Soup**
2 tablespoons cornstarch
½ teaspoon sugar
¼ teaspoon ground ginger
2 tablespoons dry sherry
1 tablespoon soy sauce
4 cups fresh or frozen **Vegetable 1**
1 cup thinly sliced carrots
**Vegetable 2**
**Garnish**

| Soup | Vegetable 1 | Vegetable 2 | Garnish |
|------|-------------|-------------|---------|
| chicken broth | cut broccoli | 2 cups fresh or frozen snow pea pods | diced tofu |
| French onion | cut asparagus | 2 cups fresh bean sprouts | sliced almonds |
| beef broth | peas | 1 can (8 ounces) sliced water chestnuts, drained | sesame seed |

1. In 10-inch skillet, combine **Soup,** cornstarch, sugar, ginger, sherry and soy sauce. Over medium heat, heat to boiling, stirring constantly. Add **Vegetable 1** and carrots. Reduce heat to low. Cover; simmer 10 minutes or until vegetables are tender, stirring occasionally.

2. Stir in **Vegetable 2.** Cook until heated through, stirring often. Sprinkle with **Garnish.** Serve with additional soy sauce. Makes about 4 cups, 6 servings.

# Tomato Vegetable Skillet

2 tablespoons salad oil
1 large onion, chopped
1 medium green pepper, cut into strips
1 clove garlic, minced
1 can (10½ to 11 ounces) condensed **Soup**
**Vegetable**
**Seasoning**
1 tablespoon lemon juice
**Cheese**

| Soup | Vegetable | Seasoning | Cheese |
|---|---|---|---|
| tomato bisque | 6 cups sliced zucchini | ½ teaspoon basil leaves, crushed | ¼ cup grated Parmesan |
| Spanish style vegetable | 6 cups cubed eggplant | ½ teaspoon oregano leaves, crushed | ½ cup crumbled feta |
| tomato | 4 cups fresh or frozen cut green beans | ½ teaspoon thyme leaves, crushed | 1 cup shredded Cheddar |
| tomato rice | 4 cups fresh or frozen sliced okra | 1 teaspoon chili powder | 1 cup shredded Monterey Jack |

1. In 10-inch skillet over medium heat, in hot oil, cook onion, green pepper and garlic until tender, stirring occasionally.

2. Stir in **Soup, Vegetable, Seasoning** and lemon juice. Heat to boiling. Reduce heat to low. Cover; simmer 5 to 15 minutes until vegetable is nearly tender, stirring occasionally. Uncover; simmer until sauce is desired consistency.

3. Sprinkle with **Cheese.** Cook 2 minutes more or until cheese is melted. Makes 6 servings.

# Onion-Vegetable Bake

1 can (10¾ to 11 ounces) condensed **Soup**
½ cup **Liquid**
1 teaspoon soy sauce
Dash pepper
4 cups drained, cooked **Vegetable**
1 can (2.8 ounces) French-fried onions

| Soup | Liquid | Vegetable |
|------|--------|-----------|
| cream of mushroom | milk | cut green beans |
| cream of celery | light cream | sliced carrots |
| cream of chicken | plain yogurt | cut broccoli |
| Cheddar cheese | sour cream | Brussels sprouts |

1. In 1½-quart casserole, combine **Soup, Liquid,** soy sauce and pepper. Stir in **Vegetable** and ½ of the onions.

2. Bake at 350°F. 25 minutes or until hot. Top with remaining onions. Bake 5 minutes more. Makes 6 servings.

*To Microwave:* In 2-quart microwave-safe casserole, combine **Soup, Liquid,** soy sauce and pepper. Stir in **Vegetable** and ½ of the onions; cover. Microwave on HIGH 4 to 7 minutes until hot, stirring once. Top with remaining onions.

**Tip:** *Buy 1 package (16 to 20 ounces) frozen vegetables, 2 packages (9 to 10 ounces each) frozen vegetables, 2 cans (about 16 ounces each) canned vegetables, or about 1½ pounds fresh vegetables for this recipe.*

# Skillet Potatoes

3 tablespoons butter or margarine
1 cup **Vegetable 1**
½ cup **Vegetable 2**
2 cloves garlic, minced
1 can (10¾ ounces) condensed chicken broth
¼ cup water
4 cups cubed potatoes
1 cup carrots cut into julienne strips
**Seasoning**
**Garnish**

| Vegetable 1 | Vegetable 2 | Seasoning | Garnish |
| --- | --- | --- | --- |
| sliced celery | chopped onion | ⅛ teaspoon pepper | chopped fresh parsley |
| frozen French-style green beans, thawed | sliced green onions with tops | ¼ teaspoon thyme leaves, crushed | chopped fresh chives |
| sliced mushrooms | chopped leeks | ⅛ teaspoon dry mustard | toasted sesame seed |
| chopped tomatoes | chopped green pepper | ⅛ teaspoon crushed red pepper | chopped pimento |

1. In 10-inch skillet over medium heat, in hot butter, cook **Vegetable 1, Vegetable 2** and garlic until vegetables are tender, stirring occasionally.

2. Add broth, water, potatoes, carrots and **Seasoning** to skillet. Heat to boiling; reduce heat to low. Cover; simmer 15 minutes or until potatoes are tender.

3. Uncover; over medium heat, simmer 5 minutes or until broth is slightly thickened, stirring often. Sprinkle with **Garnish** before serving. Makes about 5 cups, 6 servings.

**Tip:** *You may be surprised to find that this tasty potato dish contains only 140 to 150 calories per serving.*

# Broccoli and Noodles Parmesan

1 bunch broccoli (about 1½ pounds)
2 tablespoons butter or margarine
½ cup chopped onion
1 clove garlic, minced
1 can (10¾ to 11 ounces) condensed **Soup**
**Seasoning**
1 cup shredded **Cheese**
½ cup grated Parmesan cheese
1 cup **Dairy**
8 ounces (about 6 cups) noodles, cooked and drained

*Add chunks of cooked ck. breast*

| Soup | Seasoning | Cheese | Dairy |
|---|---|---|---|
| cream of mushroom | ½ teaspoon tarragon leaves, crushed | American | sour cream |
| cream of onion | ½ teaspoon basil leaves, crushed | Cheddar | plain yogurt |
| cream of chicken | ½ teaspoon curry powder | Swiss | ricotta cheese |
| Cheddar cheese | ¼ teaspoon cayenne pepper | Monterey Jack | creamed small curd cottage cheese |

1. Cut broccoli into bite-sized pieces. In covered 4-quart saucepan over medium heat, in 1 inch boiling water, cook broccoli 6 minutes or until tender. Drain in colander.

2. In same saucepan over medium heat, in hot butter, cook onion and garlic until tender, stirring occasionally. Stir in **Soup** and **Seasoning;** mix well.

3. Add **Cheese** and Parmesan, stirring until melted. Stir in **Dairy,** broccoli and cooked noodles. Pour into 2-quart casserole. Cover; bake at 350°F. 30 minutes or until bubbly. Makes 8 servings.

*To Microwave:* Cut broccoli into bite-sized pieces. In 3-quart microwave-safe casserole, combine broccoli and ½ cup water; cover. Microwave on HIGH 6 to 8 minutes until almost tender. Let stand, covered, 2 to 3 minutes. Drain in colander. In same casserole, combine butter, onion and garlic; cover. Microwave on HIGH 2 to 2½ minutes until onion is tender. Stir in **Soup, Seasoning, Cheese** and Parmesan. Stir in **Dairy,** broccoli and cooked noodles; cover. Microwave on HIGH 8 to 10 minutes until heated through, stirring occasionally. Let stand, covered, 2 to 3 minutes.

**Tip:** *To make clean-up easy, cook noodles first in 4-quart saucepan, then use it to cook broccoli, then sauce. Add broccoli to same colander with noodles to drain.*

---

# Macaroni and Cheese

1 can (10¾ to 11 ounces) condensed **Soup**
¾ cup **Liquid**
1 teaspoon prepared mustard
⅛ teaspoon pepper
6 ounces (about 1½ cups) elbow macaroni, cooked and drained
2 cups shredded **Cheese**
**Topper**

| Soup | Liquid | Cheese | Topper |
| --- | --- | --- | --- |
| cream of mushroom | milk | Cheddar | 1 cup French-fried onions |
| cream of onion | water | American | 1 cup coarsely crushed potato chips |
| cream of celery | evaporated milk | Swiss | ¼ cup buttered bread crumbs |
| Cheddar cheese | tomato juice | Monterey Jack | 1 medium tomato, sliced |

1. In 1½-quart casserole, stir together **Soup, Liquid,** mustard and pepper. Stir in macaroni and 1½ cups of the **Cheese.** Bake at 400°F. 25 minutes or until hot; stir.

2. Sprinkle with remaining ½ cup **Cheese** and **Topper;** bake 5 minutes more or until cheese melts. Makes 6 servings.

*To Microwave:* In 2-quart microwave-safe casserole, stir together **Soup, Liquid,** mustard, pepper, macaroni and 1½ cups of the **Cheese;** cover. Microwave on HIGH 7 to 10 minutes until hot, stirring occasionally. Sprinkle with remaining ½ cup **Cheese** and **Topper.** Microwave, uncovered, on HIGH 30 to 45 seconds until cheese melts.

**Tip:** *To make buttered crumbs, toss ¼ cup fine dry bread crumbs with 1 tablespoon butter or margarine, melted. You can buy dry crumbs in your supermarket, or make them at home. Bake bread slices at 300°F. about 20 minutes until very dry. Cool; crush with a rolling pin or in a blender.*

# Savory Pilaf

2 tablespoons butter or margarine
1 cup **Vegetable**
½ cup sliced green onions
1 clove garlic, minced
1 cup **Grain**
1 can (10½ to 10¾ ounces) condensed **Soup**
¾ cup water
**Seasoning**
2 tablespoons chopped fresh parsley

| Vegetable | Grain | Soup | Seasoning |
|---|---|---|---|
| shredded carrots | raw regular rice | chicken gumbo | ¼ teaspoon marjoram leaves, crushed |
| chopped green or red pepper | raw brown rice | French onion | ¼ teaspoon curry powder |
| chopped tomato | raw pearled barley | beef broth | ¼ teaspoon oregano leaves, crushed |
| chopped celery | raw bulgur wheat | chicken broth | ½ teaspoon rubbed sage |

1. In 3-quart saucepan over medium heat, in hot butter, cook **Vegetable,** green onions and garlic until tender, stirring occasionally. Stir in **Grain;** cook 5 minutes more, stirring occasionally.

2. Stir in **Soup,** water and **Seasoning.** Heat to boiling. Reduce heat to low; cover. Simmer until grain is tender (about 25 minutes for regular rice, 50 minutes for brown rice, 1 hour for barley, 15 minutes for bulgur); stir occasionally. Add more water during cooking if mixture appears dry. Garnish with parsley. Makes about 3 cups, 4 servings.

**Tip:** *Regular rice is the rice grain with its outer layer (the bran) removed. Brown rice has most of its bran intact; that's why brown rice is chewier and takes longer to cook.*

# Salads and Dressings

⚜

## Garden Pasta Salad

¼ cup salad oil
1 cup sliced mushrooms
½ cup chopped onion
1 clove garlic, minced
1 cup **Vegetable 1**
**Vegetable 2**
1 teaspoon basil leaves, crushed
4 ounces **Macaroni,** cooked and drained
¼ cup sliced pitted ripe olives
1 can (10½ ounces) condensed Spanish style vegetable soup
¼ cup red wine vinegar
**Cheese**

| Vegetable 1 | Vegetable 2 | Macaroni | Cheese |
|---|---|---|---|
| thinly sliced zucchini | 1 cup broccoli cut into bite-sized pieces | corkscrews | 1 cup cubed Muenster |
| fresh or frozen cut green beans | 1 can (8 ounces) red kidney beans, drained | sea shells | 1 cup cubed Provolone |
| fresh or frozen cut asparagus | 1 cup diagonally sliced carrots | elbows | ¼ cup crumbled blue cheese |
| fresh or frozen snow pea pods | 1 cup cauliflower cut into bite-sized pieces | wagon wheels | ⅓ cup grated Parmesan |

1. In 10-inch skillet over medium heat, in hot oil, cook mushrooms, onion and garlic about 5 minutes until tender, stirring occasionally.

2. Stir in **Vegetable 1, Vegetable 2** and basil. Cover; cook 5 minutes or until vegetables are tender-crisp, stirring occasionally. Remove from heat.

3. In large bowl, toss together vegetable mixture, cooked **Macaroni,** olives, soup and vinegar. Cover; refrigerate until serving time, at least 4 hours. Just before serving, add **Cheese;** toss lightly. Makes about 5 cups, 6 servings.

# Blue Ribbon Carrot Salad

2 pounds carrots, cut into 2 by ¼-inch sticks
1 can (10¾ ounces) condensed tomato soup
¼ cup sugar
½ cup vinegar
¼ cup salad oil
1 teaspoon **Seasoning**
1 teaspoon Worcestershire
**Vegetable 1**
**Vegetable 2**

| Seasoning | Vegetable 1 | Vegetable 2 |
|---|---|---|
| prepared mustard | 1 cup<br>sliced celery | 1 cup fresh snow pea pods,<br>halved crosswise,<br>cooked and drained |
| dry mustard | 1 medium onion,<br>sliced | 1 green pepper,<br>cut into strips |
| prepared horseradish | ½ cup<br>sliced radishes | 1 cup drained,<br>cooked cut green beans |
| chili powder | ½ cup<br>sliced green onions | 1 medium cucumber,<br>halved lengthwise and sliced |

1. In 4-quart saucepan over medium heat, in 1 inch boiling water, cook carrots until tender. Drain; cool slightly.

2. In large bowl, combine soup, sugar, vinegar, oil, **Seasoning** and Worcestershire.

3. Add cooked carrots, **Vegetable 1** and **Vegetable 2;** toss to coat well. Cover; refrigerate until serving time, at least 4 hours. Makes about 6 cups, 8 servings.

*To Microwave:* In 2-quart microwave-safe casserole, combine carrots and ¼ cup water; cover. Microwave on HIGH 8 to 12 minutes until tender, stirring twice. Let stand, covered, 2 minutes. Drain; cool slightly. Proceed as in Steps 2 and 3.

**Tip:** *The dressing on this salad also makes a delicious marinade for broiled or grilled meats.*

# Buffet Layered Salad

1 can (10¾ ounces) condensed **Soup**
1 cup **Base**
¼ cup grated Parmesan cheese
1 tablespoon grated onion
6 cups torn salad greens
2 medium **Vegetables,** thinly sliced
2 cups sliced mushrooms
2 medium tomatoes, diced
½ cup chopped green onions
**Garnish**

| Soup | Base | Vegetables | Garnish |
|------|------|------------|---------|
| cream of mushroom | sour cream | carrots | sliced pitted ripe olives |
| cream of celery | plain yogurt | zucchini | chopped fresh parsley |
| cream of chicken | mayonnaise | cucumbers | chopped hard-cooked egg |

1. For dressing, in medium bowl, combine **Soup, Base,** cheese and onion. Mix until smooth; set aside.

2. In clear 4-quart bowl, layer salad greens, **Vegetables,** mushrooms and tomatoes. Spoon dressing over salad, spreading to cover salad. Cover; refrigerate until serving time, at least 4 hours.

3. Sprinkle with green onions and **Garnish** before serving. Makes 12 servings.

**Tip:** *Use your favorite salad greens. Choose a mixture of iceberg, Boston, Bibb, romaine, butter, leaf and red-tipped lettuces, as well as spinach, endive, arugula, radicchio, watercress and parsley.*

# Potato Salad

3 pounds potatoes
1 can (10¾ ounces) condensed **Soup**
¾ cup mayonnaise
2 tablespoons red wine vinegar
**Seasoning**
1 cup chopped celery
**Vegetable 1**
½ cup **Vegetable 2**
2 hard-cooked eggs, chopped

| Soup | Seasoning | Vegetable 1 | Vegetable 2 |
|------|-----------|-------------|-------------|
| cream of celery | ⅛ teaspoon pepper | ¾ cup drained, cooked peas | sliced radishes |
| cream of chicken | ¼ teaspoon dry mustard | ¼ cup chopped green onions | chopped cucumber |
| cream of onion | ½ teaspoon celery seed | ½ cup drained, cooked diced carrot | chopped green pepper |
| cream of mushroom | ⅛ teaspoon cayenne pepper | ½ cup diced zucchini | sliced pitted ripe olives |

1. In 4-quart saucepan, place potatoes; add water to cover. Over high heat, heat to boiling. Reduce heat to low; cover. Simmer 20 to 30 minutes until fork-tender; drain. Cool slightly. Peel potatoes; cut potatoes into ½-inch cubes.

2. In large bowl, mix together **Soup,** mayonnaise, vinegar and **Seasoning** until well blended.

3. Add potatoes, celery, **Vegetable 1, Vegetable 2** and eggs; toss gently to mix. Cover; refrigerate until serving time, at least 4 hours. Makes about 7 cups, 8 servings.

**Tip:** *Choose red potatoes or other round potato varieties for making potato salad. Or, cook small new potatoes for this salad, then halve them instead of cutting into cubes.*

# Tomato French Dressing

1 can (10¾ ounces) condensed tomato soup
½ cup salad oil
¼ cup **Liquid**
**Seasoning**
**Flavoring**

| Liquid | Seasoning | Flavoring |
|---|---|---|
| cider vinegar | ½ teaspoon dry mustard | 4 slices bacon, cooked, drained and crumbled |
| lemon juice | 1 tablespoon grated onion | ¼ cup crumbled blue cheese |
| wine vinegar | 1 tablespoon finely chopped green onion | 1 clove garlic, minced |

In covered jar or shaker, combine all ingredients; shake well before using. Serve over mixed salad greens or fruit salads. Makes about 2 cups.

# Creamy Salad Dressing

1 can (10¾ to 11 ounces) condensed **Soup**
½ cup mayonnaise
⅓ cup chopped fresh parsley
**Liquid**
**Seasoning**
**Flavoring**
⅛ teaspoon pepper

| Soup | Liquid | Seasoning | Flavoring |
|---|---|---|---|
| cream of asparagus | ¼ cup tarragon vinegar | 3 green onions, thinly sliced | 2 tablespoons finely chopped anchovies |
| cream of onion | 1 tablespoon tomato paste | 3 tablespoons sweet pickle relish | 1 hard-cooked egg, chopped |
| cream of mushroom | 3 to 4 tablespoons lemon juice | ⅓ cup grated Parmesan cheese | 2 cloves garlic, minced |
| Cheddar cheese | ¼ cup buttermilk | 2 slices bacon, cooked, drained and crumbled | 1 tablespoon Worcestershire |

In small bowl, combine **Soup** and mayonnaise; mix until smooth. Add remaining ingredients; mix well. Cover; refrigerate until serving time, at least 4 hours. Serve over mixed salad greens. Makes about 2 cups.

# *Sauces*

❦

# Sweet and Sour Sauce

⅓ cup **Sweetener**
2 tablespoons cornstarch
**Spice**
1 clove garlic, minced
1 can (10¾ ounces) condensed chicken broth
⅓ cup cider vinegar
1 to 2 teaspoons soy sauce
¼ cup **Vegetable**
**Fruit**

| Sweetener | Spice | Vegetable | Fruit |
|---|---|---|---|
| sugar | ¼ teaspoon ground nutmeg | sliced water chestnuts | 1 can (8 ounces) mandarin orange segments, drained |
| honey | 6 whole cloves | green onions cut into 1-inch pieces | 1 cup pineapple chunks |
| apple jelly | 1 stick cinnamon | zucchini cut into julienne strips | ½ cup halved cherry tomatoes |
| packed brown sugar | ⅛ teaspoon minced fresh ginger root | green pepper cut into julienne strips | 1 can (8 ounces) apricot halves, drained and cut up |

1. In 2-quart saucepan, combine **Sweetener,** cornstarch, **Spice** and garlic. Gradually stir in broth, vinegar and soy sauce. Over medium-high heat, heat to boiling, stirring constantly; boil 1 minute. Discard cloves or cinnamon stick.

2. Stir in **Vegetable** and **Fruit;** heat through. Serve over fish, poultry or meat. Makes about 2 cups.

# Souper Gravy

Drippings from roast meat or poultry
1 can (10¾ ounces) condensed **Soup**
**Liquid**
**Seasoning 1**
**Seasoning 2**

| Soup | Liquid | Seasoning 1 | Seasoning 2 |
|---|---|---|---|
| golden mushroom | ¼ cup milk | ¼ teaspoon tarragon leaves, crushed | 1 tablespoon chopped fresh chives |
| cream of onion | ¼ cup water | 1 teaspoon Worcestershire | ¼ teaspoon marjoram leaves, crushed |
| cream of chicken | ¼ cup sour cream plus ⅓ cup water | ½ teaspoon soy sauce | 1 tablespoon chopped green onion |
| cream of celery | 2 tablespoons dry sherry plus 2 tablespoons water | ⅛ teaspoon ground nutmeg | ½ cup cooked or canned sliced mushrooms |

1. Remove roast from pan. Pour off pan drippings, reserving 2 tablespoons in pan.

2. Pour **Soup** into roasting pan; stir well to loosen brown bits. Blend in **Liquid.** Add **Seasoning 1** and **Seasoning 2.** Over medium heat, heat through, stirring often. Serve with meat or poultry. Makes about 1½ cups.

**Tip:** *If you do not have drippings, substitute 2 tablespoons butter or margarine. In 2-quart saucepan over medium heat, melt butter; stir in remaining ingredients. Heat through.*

# Cream Sauce

1 can (10¾ ounces) condensed **Soup**
**Liquid**
**Flavoring**
**Seasoning**

| Soup | Liquid | Flavoring | Seasoning |
|---|---|---|---|
| cream of celery | ⅓ cup water plus 2 tablespoons dry sherry | ½ cup shredded Swiss cheese | 2 tablespoons grated Parmesan cheese |
| cream of onion | ½ cup water | ½ cup sour cream | ⅛ teaspoon paprika |
| cream of mushroom | ½ cup milk | ½ cup cooked or canned sliced mushrooms | 2 teaspoons chopped fresh chives |
| cream of chicken | ½ cup light cream | 2 tablespoons chopped fresh parsley | ¼ teaspoon tarragon leaves, crushed |

In 2-quart saucepan, combine all ingredients. Over medium heat, heat through, stirring frequently. Serve over vegetables. Makes about 1½ cups.

*To Microwave:* In 1-quart microwave-safe casserole, combine all ingredients; cover. Microwave on HIGH 5 to 7 minutes until hot, stirring occasionally.

Tip: *When you use a condensed cream soup to make a sauce, you don't need to worry about lumps because the flour is thoroughly cooked before you open the can. Any leftover sauce can be refrigerated and reheated later; thin it with a little water or milk if it becomes too thick.*

# No-Cook Spicy Barbecue Sauce

1 can (10¾ ounces) condensed tomato soup
**Liquid**
2 tablespoons **Sweetener**
2 tablespoons Worcestershire
**Seasoning**
1 teaspoon dry mustard

| Liquid | Sweetener | Seasoning |
|--------|-----------|-----------|
| ¼ cup cider vinegar | brown sugar | 2 teaspoons chili powder |
| ⅓ cup lemon juice | honey | ½ teaspoon hot pepper sauce |
| ⅓ cup lime juice | grape jam | 2 teaspoons curry powder |
| ¼ cup red wine vinegar | molasses | ½ teaspoon ground ginger |

In medium bowl, combine all ingredients; stir well. Use to baste chicken, spareribs, lamb, hamburgers or turkey. Makes about 1½ cups.

# Curry Sauce

2 tablespoons butter or margarine
¼ cup chopped onion
2 teaspoons curry powder
1 can (10¾ ounces) condensed **Soup**
½ cup **Liquid**
½ cup **Fruit**
**Garnish**

| Soup | Liquid | Fruit | Garnish |
|------|--------|-------|---------|
| tomato | chicken broth | chopped tomato | raisins |
| cream of celery | apple juice | chopped apple | salted peanuts |
| cream of chicken | water | chopped pear | cashews |
| cream of mushroom | pineapple juice | drained crushed pineapple | toasted flaked coconut |

1. In 2-quart saucepan over medium heat, in hot butter, cook onion and curry until onion is tender, stirring occasionally.

2. Stir in **Soup** and **Liquid** until well blended. Add **Fruit;** heat through, stirring occasionally. Top with **Garnish.** Serve over meat, poultry or rice. Makes about 2 cups.

# Cheese Sauce

1 can (10¾ to 11 ounces) condensed **Soup**
**Liquid**
**Cheese**
**Seasoning**

| Soup | Liquid | Cheese | Seasoning |
|---|---|---|---|
| cream of celery | ⅓ cup milk | 1½ cups shredded sharp Cheddar | ½ teaspoon dry mustard |
| cream of mushroom | 2 tablespoons sherry plus ⅓ cup milk | 1 package (3 ounces) cream cheese, cubed | 1 tablespoon Worcestershire |
| cream of onion | ½ cup sour cream plus ⅓ cup milk | ½ cup grated Parmesan | 1 tablespoon chopped fresh parsley |
| Cheddar cheese | ⅓ cup beer | 1½ cups shredded Swiss | dash ground nutmeg |

In 2-quart saucepan, combine all ingredients. Over medium heat, heat through, stirring frequently. Serve over vegetables, hamburgers or pasta. Makes about 2 cups.

*To Microwave:* In 1-quart microwave-safe casserole, combine all ingredients; stir to blend well. Cover. Microwave on HIGH 4 to 6 minutes until hot, stirring occasionally.

**Tip:** *This is a terrific sauce for serving over split baked potatoes. Make them into a main dish by topping with broccoli flowerets, chili, crumbled bacon or your own favorite additions before adding the cheese sauce.*

# Carbonara Sauce

1 can (10¾ ounces) condensed **Soup**
**Meat**
**Flavoring**
½ cup half-and-half
**Cheese**

| Soup | Meat | Flavoring | Cheese |
| --- | --- | --- | --- |
| cream of onion | 6 slices bacon, cooked, drained and crumbled | ¼ cup chopped parsley | 2 tablespoons grated Romano |
| cream of celery | ½ pound bulk pork sausage, cooked, drained and crumbled | 2 tablespoons chopped green onions | 2 tablespoons grated Parmesan |
| cream of shrimp | 1 cup diced cooked ham | ¼ cup chopped green pepper | ¼ cup grated Gruyère |
| cream of mushroom | ½ cup diced prosciutto | 2 tablespoons chopped fresh basil leaves | ½ cup shredded Swiss |

1. In 2-quart saucepan over medium heat, heat **Soup, Meat, Flavoring** and half-and-half until hot, stirring frequently.

2. Stir in **Cheese** until melted. Serve over hot cooked pasta. Makes about 2 cups, 4 servings.

*To Microwave:* In 1-quart microwave-safe casserole, combine **Soup, Meat, Flavoring** and half-and-half; cover. Microwave on HIGH 4 to 6 minutes until hot, stirring once. Stir in **Cheese** until melted.

**Tip:** *Prosciutto is salted but not smoked, aged Italian ham that you can buy in your supermarket delicatessen. Have it sliced thinly, then cut it into small pieces for this recipe.*

# *Soup Surprises*

## ⚜

# No-Knead Onion Bread

**Flour**
2 tablespoons sugar
2 packages active dry yeast
1 can (10½ ounces) condensed French onion soup
¼ cup butter or margarine
1 egg
1 cup **Cheese**
1 tablespoon water
2 teaspoons **Topping**

| Flour | Cheese | Topping |
|---|---|---|
| 3 cups all-purpose | grated Romano | sesame seed |
| 1 cup rye plus 2 cups all-purpose | shredded Cheddar | poppy seed |
| 1½ cups whole wheat plus 1½ cups all-purpose | shredded American | minced dried onion |

1. In large bowl, combine 1 cup of the **Flour,** sugar and yeast.

2. In small saucepan over medium heat, heat soup and butter until very warm (120° to 130°F.). Butter does not need to melt completely.

3. With mixer at low speed, gradually pour soup mixture into dry ingredients, mixing well. At medium speed, beat 3 minutes or until smooth. Add egg, **Cheese** and 1 cup of the **Flour;** beat 2 minutes more.

4. With spoon, stir in enough remaining **Flour** to make a stiff batter. Cover; let rise in warm place until doubled, about 1½ hours.

5. Grease 1½-quart casserole. Stir down batter. Turn into casserole. Cover; let rise until doubled, about 45 minutes. Preheat oven to 325°F.

6. Brush with water and sprinkle with **Topping.** Bake 50 minutes or until bread sounds hollow when tapped with finger. Remove from pan; cool on wire rack before slicing. Makes 1 loaf, 16 servings.

**Tip:** *When using a mixture of flours, stir flours together well before using. If you need any additional flour, use all-purpose.*

---

# Cheese-Topped Sandwich Stacks

4 English muffins, split and toasted
8 slices bacon, halved, cooked and drained
1⅓ cups **Vegetable 1**
8 ounces **Meat**
**Vegetable 2**
1 can (10¾ to 11 ounces) condensed **Soup**
¼ cup milk
1½ cups shredded Cheddar cheese
1 tablespoon Worcestershire
½ teaspoon dry mustard

| Vegetable 1 | Meat | Vegetable 2 | Soup |
|---|---|---|---|
| shredded lettuce | thinly sliced cooked ham | 8 slices tomato | cream of mushroom |
| bean sprouts | thinly sliced cooked turkey | 1 avocado, sliced | cream of chicken |
| alfalfa sprouts | thinly sliced roast beef | hot pickled peppers | Cheddar cheese |

1. Place toasted English muffins on baking sheet. Top each half with bacon, **Vegetable 1, Meat** and **Vegetable 2.** Set aside.

2. In 2-quart saucepan, combine **Soup** and milk. Over medium heat, heat through, stirring occasionally. Add cheese, Worcestershire and dry mustard. Heat until cheese melts, stirring constantly. Pour sauce over each muffin.

3. Broil 4 inches from heat 1 to 2 minutes until tops start to brown. Makes 4 servings.

**Tip:** *For a lighter meal, just make the sauce in this recipe as described in step 2, then serve over toast or toasted English muffins as you would serve Welsh rarebit.*

# Scrambled Eggs in Pita Pockets

4 pita bread rounds, halved
8 eggs
1 can (10¾ ounces) condensed **Soup**
1 cup **Vegetable**
**Meat**
2 tablespoons butter or margarine
1 cup shredded **Cheese**

| Soup | Vegetable | Meat | Cheese |
|---|---|---|---|
| cream of mushroom | sliced mushrooms | 6 slices bacon, diced | Cheddar |
| cream of celery | diced tomatoes | 1 cup diced cooked ham plus 2 tablespoons salad oil | American |
| cream of chicken | chopped green pepper | ¼ pound bulk pork sausage | Monterey Jack |
| cream of onion | diced zucchini | ¼ pound pepperoni, diced | Muenster |

1. Wrap pita bread in aluminum foil; bake at 350°F. 15 minutes or until warm.

2. Meanwhile, in bowl with whisk or rotary beater, beat eggs until foamy. Stir in **Soup** and **Vegetable;** set aside.

3. In 10-inch skillet over medium heat, cook bacon or pork sausage until done, or cook ham or pepperoni until heated through, stirring occasionally. Pour off fat.

4. Add butter to skillet; heat until foamy. Add egg mixture; cook until set but still slightly moist, stirring and lifting eggs so uncooked portion flows to bottom.

5. Stuff warm pita pockets with egg mixture. Add **Cheese** to each. Makes 8 servings.

**Tip:** *Buy pita bread rounds in the bakery or delicatessen section of your supermarket. They are usually available in white and whole wheat varieties. Cut them in half crosswise for stuffing.*

# Sausage Breakfast Bake

12 ounces **Sausage**
2 tablespoons water
1 can (10¾ to 11 ounces) condensed **Soup**
2 eggs
¾ cup **Liquid**
2 tablespoons salad oil
1 cup all-purpose flour
1 cup cornmeal
¼ cup sugar
1 tablespoon baking powder
Butter or margarine
**Topping**

| Sausage | Soup | Liquid | Topping |
|---------|------|--------|---------|
| pork sausage links | cream of mushroom | apple juice | honey |
| smoked sausage links | Cheddar cheese | milk | maple syrup |
| Italian sausage in casings, cut into 2-inch lengths | cream of celery | chicken broth | fruit preserves |

1. Preheat oven to 350°F. Grease 12 by 8-inch baking dish.

2. In covered 10-inch skillet over medium heat, cook **Sausage** in water 5 minutes. Uncover; cook until sausages are browned, turning occasionally. Drain on paper towels.

3. In small bowl, combine **Soup** and eggs; stir to mix well. Gradually stir in **Liquid** and oil; mix until smooth.

4. In medium bowl, combine flour, cornmeal, sugar and baking powder. Add soup mixture, stirring just to moisten. Pour into prepared baking dish. Arrange sausages on batter.

5. Bake 30 minutes or until bread springs back when lightly touched with finger. Serve warm with butter and **Topping**. Makes 6 servings.

# Fruited Spice Cake Squares

1 package (2-layer size) spice cake mix
1 can (10¾ ounces) condensed tomato soup
½ cup water
2 eggs
1 cup **Fruit**
½ cup butter or margarine, softened
3 cups confectioners' sugar
1 teaspoon **Flavoring**
3 tablespoons **Liquid**
1 cup **Topping**

| Fruit | Flavoring | Liquid | Topping |
|---|---|---|---|
| raisins | grated orange peel | orange juice | finely chopped walnuts |
| chopped dried apricots | vanilla extract | milk | granola |
| chopped prunes | grated lemon peel | apple juice | toasted flaked coconut |

1. Preheat oven to 350°F. Grease 15 by 10-inch jelly-roll pan.

2. Mix cake mix, tomato soup, water and eggs, following directions on package. Fold in **Fruit.** Pour batter into prepared pan.

3. Bake 25 to 30 minutes until toothpick inserted in cake comes out clean. Cool completely in pan on wire rack.

4. In medium bowl, beat butter until creamy. Gradually add confectioners' sugar, **Flavoring** and **Liquid,** stirring until smooth. Spread on cake; sprinkle with **Topping.** Cut cake into squares. Makes 24 squares.

**Tip:** *This cake can be baked in two greased 9 by 5-inch loaf pans at 350°F. 45 minutes. Cool in pans 10 minutes, then cool completely on wire racks before frosting. Slice to serve.*

# Spicy Vegetable Cake

2 cups all-purpose flour
1⅓ cups packed brown sugar
2 teaspoons baking powder
1 teaspoon baking soda
Ground **Spice**
1 can (10¾ ounces) condensed tomato soup
½ cup shortening
2 eggs
¼ cup **Syrup**
1 cup shredded **Vegetable**
½ cup **Addition**

| Spice | Syrup | Vegetable | Addition |
|---|---|---|---|
| 1 teaspoon allspice plus 1 teaspoon nutmeg plus 1 teaspoon cinnamon | molasses | carrots | raisins |
| 1½ teaspoons ginger plus ½ teaspoon cloves plus ½ teaspoon cinnamon | honey | zucchini | flaked coconut |
| 1 tablespoon pumpkin pie spice | maple-flavored syrup | peeled sweet potatoes | chopped nuts |

1. Preheat oven to 350°F. Grease 10-inch tube pan.

2. In large bowl, combine flour, brown sugar, baking powder, baking soda and **Spice.** Add soup and shortening. With mixer at medium speed, beat 2 minutes, constantly scraping sides and bottom of bowl.

3. Add eggs and **Syrup;** beat 2 minutes more. Fold in **Vegetable** and **Addition.** Turn into prepared pan; bake about 1 hour until toothpick inserted in cake comes out clean. Cool in pan on rack 10 minutes. Remove from pan; cool completely. Serve plain or topped with whipped cream. Makes 16 servings.

**Tip:** *This cake can be baked in a greased and floured 13 by 9-inch baking pan at 350°F. 40 to 50 minutes. Or, bake in two greased and floured 9-inch round cake pans at 350°F. 30 to 35 minutes. Layer cooled cakes with whipped cream.*

# Souper Cheesecake

1 cup **Crumbs**
¼ cup butter or margarine, melted
12 ounces cream cheese, softened
⅔ cup sugar
3 eggs
1 can (11 ounces) condensed Cheddar cheese soup
**Flavoring 1**
**Flavoring 2**
**Topping**

| Crumbs | Flavoring 1 | Flavoring 2 | Topping |
|---|---|---|---|
| graham cracker | 1 teaspoon grated lemon peel | 2 tablespoons lemon juice | fresh strawberries |
| zwieback | 2 teaspoons grated orange peel | 2 tablespoons orange juice | fresh blueberries |
| gingersnap | 1 teaspoon pumpkin pie spice | 2 teaspoons vanilla extract | canned cherry pie filling |
| vanilla wafer | 3 ounces semisweet chocolate, melted | 2 tablespoons coffee liqueur | sweetened whipped cream |

1. In small bowl, combine **Crumbs** and butter; mix well. Press crumb mixture into bottom of 9-inch springform pan to make an even layer. Set aside.

2. In large bowl with mixer at medium speed, beat cream cheese until smooth. Alternately add sugar and eggs, beating well after each addition. Beat in soup, **Flavoring 1** and **Flavoring 2** until blended. Pour over crust.

3. Bake at 350°F. 1 hour or until puffed around edges and set in center. Cool completely in pan on wire rack. Refrigerate until serving time, at least 4 hours. Garnish with **Topping**. Makes 12 servings.

**Tip:** *To make a cheese pie, prepare filling as above in step 2; pour into 9-inch unbaked piecrust. Bake at 350°F. 45 minutes or until set in center. Cool, chill and garnish as above.*

# Index

## A
**Appetizers**
Appetizer Cheesecake, 4
Avocado Dip, 6
Cheese Ball, 6
Cheese-Stuffed
Vegetables, 8
French Pizza Slices, 13
Mexican-Style Appetizer,
10
Rumaki Spread, 7
Tomato Cheese Fondue,
12
**Asparagus**
Extra-Good Cream Soup,
19
Garden Pasta Salad, 68
Vegetables Oriental, 58
Avocado Dip, 6

## B
**Bacon**
Carbonara Sauce, 83
Cheese-Topped Sandwich
Stacks, 86
Pasta and Bean Soup, 16
Rumaki Spread, 7
Scrambled Eggs in Pita
Pockets, 87
Souper Easy Quiche, 54
Speedy Potato Chowder,
20
Baked Chicken Florida, 44
Barbecue Sauce, No-
Cook Spicy, 80
**Barley**
Savory Pilaf, 67
**Beans** (see also Green beans)
Garden Pasta Salad, 68
Pasta and Bean Soup, 16
**Beef**
Cheese-Topped Sandwich
Stacks, 86
Easy Pot Roast, 28
Garden Swiss Steak, 29
Souper Enchiladas, 38
Stir-Fried Beef and
Vegetables, 30
Tacos, 36
Teriyaki Beef Kabobs, 32
**Beef (ground)**
Best-Ever Meat Loaf, 33
Chili, 14

Meatball Stew, 40
Stuffed Cabbage Leaves,
34
Tacos, 36
Best-Ever Meat Loaf, 33
Blue Ribbon Carrot Salad, 70
**Breads**
No-Knead Onion Bread,
84
Sausage Breakfast Bake,
88
**Broccoli**
Broccoli and Noodles
Parmesan, 64
Garden Pasta Salad, 68
Onion-Vegetable Bake, 61
Vegetable Lasagna, 49
Vegetables Oriental, 58
**Brown rice**
Savory Pilaf, 67
**Brussels sprouts**
Onion-Vegetable Bake, 61
Buffet Layered Salad, 72
**Bulgur**
Savory Pilaf, 67

## C
Cabbage Leaves, Stuffed, 34
**Cakes**
Fruited Spice Cake
Squares, 90
Souper Cheesecake, 92
Spicy Vegetable Cake, 91
Carbonara Sauce, 83
**Carrots**
Blue Ribbon Carrot Salad,
70
Garden Pasta Salad, 68
Onion-Vegetable Bake, 61
Spicy Vegetable Cake, 91
**Cauliflower**
Garden Pasta Salad, 68
**Celery**
Extra-Good Cream Soup,
19
**Cheese**
Appetizer Cheesecake, 4
Broccoli and Noodles
Parmesan, 64
Cheese Ball, 6
Cheese Sauce, 82
Cheese-Stuffed
Vegetables, 8

Cheese-Topped Sandwich
Stacks, 86
Easy Soufflé, 56
Macaroni and Cheese, 66
Souper Cheesecake, 92
Souper Easy Quiche, 54
Tomato Cheese Fondue,
12
Vegetable Lasagna, 49
**Cheesecakes**
Appetizer Cheesecake, 4
Souper Cheesecake, 92
**Chicken**
Baked Chicken Florida, 44
Chicken Breasts in
Mushroom Sauce, 43
Chicken Paprika, 42
Chicken-Stuffing Bake, 48
Souper Easy Quiche, 54
Souper Enchiladas, 38
Speedy Potato Chowder,
20
Supper à la King, 46
**Chicken livers**
Rumaki Spread, 7
Chili, 14
**Clams**
Fish Stew, 24
Pasta with White Seafood
Sauce, 53
Skillet Seafood Bisque, 22
Cream Sauce, 79
Creamy Salad Dressing, 75
Curry Sauce, 80

## D
**Desserts**
Fruited Spice Cake
Squares, 90
Souper Cheesecake, 92
Spicy Vegetable Cake, 91
**Dips and spreads**
Avocado Dip, 6
Cheese Ball, 6
Mexican-Style Appetizer,
10
Rumaki Spread, 7

## E
Easy Pea Soup, 18
Easy Pot Roast, 28
Easy Soufflé, 56

**Eggplant**
Tomato Vegetable Skillet, 60
**Eggs**
Easy Soufflé, 56
Scrambled Eggs in Pita Pockets, 87
Souper Easy Quiche, 54
Enchiladas, Souper, 38
Extra-Good Cream Soup, 19

**F**
**Fish** (*see also* Tuna, Salmon)
Fish Stew, 24
Perfect Tuna Casserole, 52
Skillet Seafood Bisque, 22
Vegetable-Stuffed Fish Rolls, 50
Fondue, Tomato Cheese, 12
**Frankfurters**
Speedy Potato Chowder, 20
French Pizza Slices, 13
Fruited Chops, 26
Fruited Spice Cake Squares, 90

**G**
Garden Pasta Salad, 68
Garden Swiss Steak, 29
Gravy, Souper, 78
**Green beans**
Garden Pasta Salad, 68
Onion-Vegetable Bake, 61
Tomato Vegetable Skillet, 60
Vegetable Lasagna, 49

**H**
**Ham**
Carbonara Sauce, 83
Cheese-Topped Sandwich Stacks, 86
Pasta and Bean Soup, 16
Scrambled Eggs in Pita Pockets, 87
Souper Easy Quiche, 54
Speedy Potato Chowder, 20
Supper à la King, 46

**K**
Kabobs, Teriyaki Beef, 32
**Kielbasa**
Supper à la King, 46

**L**
**Lamb**
Fruited Chops, 26
Stuffed Cabbage Leaves, 34
Lasagna, Vegetable, 49
**Livers**
Rumaki Spread, 7

**M**
Macaroni and Cheese, 66
Meatball Stew, 40
Meat Loaf, Best-Ever, 33
Mexican-Style Appetizer, 10
**Microwave recipes**
Blue Ribbon Carrot Salad, 70
Broccoli and Noodles Parmesan, 64
Carbonara Sauce, 83
Cheese Sauce, 82
Chicken-Stuffing Bake, 48
Chili, 14
Cream Sauce, 79
Easy Pea Soup, 18
Extra-Good Cream Soup, 19
Macaroni and Cheese, 66
Onion-Vegetable Bake, 61
Perfect Tuna Casserole, 52
Souper Enchiladas, 38
Speedy Potato Chowder, 20
Supper à la King, 46
Tacos, 36
Tomato Cheese Fondue, 12
Vegetable-Stuffed Fish Rolls, 50
**Mushrooms**
Chicken Breasts in Mushroom Sauce, 43
Extra-Good Cream Soup, 19

**N**
No-Cook Spicy Barbecue Sauce, 80
No-Knead Onion Bread, 84
Noodles Parmesan, Broccoli and, 64

**O**
**Onions**
No-Knead Onion Bread, 84
Onion-Vegetable Bake, 61

**P**
Paprika, Chicken, 42
**Pasta**
Broccoli and Noodles Parmesan, 64
Garden Pasta Salad, 68
Macaroni and Cheese, 66
Pasta and Bean Soup, 16
Pasta with White Seafood Sauce, 53
Vegetable Lasagna, 49
**Peas**
Easy Pea Soup, 18
Vegetables Oriental, 58
**Pepperoni**
Scrambled Eggs in Pita Pockets, 87
Perfect Tuna Casserole, 52
Pilaf, Savory, 67
Pizza Slices, French, 13
**Pork** (*see also* Bacon, Ham, Sausage)
Best-Ever Meat Loaf, 33
Chili, 14
Fruited Chops, 26
Souper Enchiladas, 38
Stuffed Cabbage Leaves, 34
Tacos, 36
**Potatoes**
Potato Salad, 74
Skillet Potatoes, 62
Speedy Potato Chowder, 20
Pot Roast, Easy, 28

**Q**
Quiche, Souper Easy, 54

**R**
**Rice**
Savory Pilaf, 67
Rumaki Spread, 7

**S**
**Salad dressings**
Creamy Salad Dressing, 75
Tomato French Dressing, 75
**Salads**
Blue Ribbon Carrot Salad, 70

Buffet Layered Salad, 72
Garden Pasta Salad, 68
Potato Salad, 74
**Salmon**
  Pasta with White Seafood
    Sauce, 53
**Sandwiches**
  Cheese-Topped Sandwich
    Stacks, 86
  Scrambled Eggs in Pita
    Pockets, 87
**Sauces**
  Carbonara Sauce, 83
  Cheese Sauce, 82
  Cream Sauce, 79
  Curry Sauce, 80
  No-Cook Spicy Barbecue
    Sauce, 80
  Sweet and Sour Sauce, 76
**Sausage** (see also
    Frankfurters, Kielbasa)
  Best-Ever Meat Loaf, 33
  Carbonara Sauce, 83
  Chili, 14
  French Pizza Slices, 13
  Pasta and Bean Soup, 16
  Sausage Breakfast Bake,
    88
  Scrambled Eggs in Pita
    Pockets, 87
  Tacos, 36
Savory Pilaf, 67
**Scallops**
  Skillet Seafood Bisque, 22
Scrambled Eggs in Pita
  Pockets, 87
**Seafood**
  Fish Stew, 24
  Pasta with White Seafood
    Sauce, 53
  Skillet Seafood Bisque, 22
**Shrimp**
  Fish Stew, 24
  Pasta with White Seafood
    Sauce, 53
  Skillet Seafood Bisque, 22
Skillet Potatoes, 62
Skillet Seafood Bisque, 22
**Snow pea pods**
  Garden Pasta Salad, 68

Vegetables Oriental, 58
Soufflé, Easy, 56
Souper Cheesecake, 92
Souper Easy Quiche, 54
Souper Enchiladas, 38
Souper Gravy, 78
Soup Mates, 25
**Soups**
  Chili, 14
  Easy Pea Soup, 18
  Extra-Good Cream Soup,
    19
  Fish Stew, 24
  Pasta and Bean Soup, 16
  Skillet Seafood Bisque, 22
  Soup Mates, 25
  Speedy Potato Chowder,
    20
Speedy Potato Chowder, 20
Spicy Vegetable Cake, 91
**Spinach**
  Vegetable Lasagna, 49
**Spreads**
  Cheese Ball, 6
  Mexican-Style Appetizer,
    10
  Rumaki Spread, 7
**Squash** (see also Zucchini)
  Supper à la King, 46
**Stews**
  Fish Stew, 24
  Meatball Stew, 40
Stir-Fried Beef and
  Vegetables, 30
Stuffed Cabbage Leaves, 34
Stuffing Bake, Chicken-, 48
Supper à la King, 46
Sweet and Sour Sauce, 76
**Sweet potatoes**
  Spicy Vegetable Cake, 91
Swiss Steak, Garden, 29

**T**
Tacos, 36
Teriyaki Beef Kabobs, 32
**Tomatoes**
  Extra-Good Cream Soup,
    19
  Tomato Cheese Fondue,
    12

Tomato French Dressing,
  75
Tomato Vegetable Skillet,
  60
**Tuna**
  Pasta with White Seafood
    Sauce, 53
  Perfect Tuna Casserole, 52
  Speedy Potato Chowder,
    20
**Turkey**
  Cheese-Topped Sandwich
    Stacks, 86
  Chicken-Stuffing Bake, 48
  Souper Easy Quiche, 54
  Supper à la King, 46

**V**
**Veal**
  Best-Ever Meat Loaf, 33
  Fruited Chops, 26
**Vegetables** (see also individual
    listings)
  Broccoli and Noodles
    Parmesan, 64
  Cheese-Stuffed
    Vegetables, 8
  Onion-Vegetable Bake, 61
  Skillet Potatoes, 62
  Spicy Vegetable Cake, 91
  Stir-Fried Beef and
    Vegetables, 30
  Tomato Vegetable Skillet,
    60
  Vegetable Lasagna, 49
  Vegetables Oriental, 58
  Vegetable-Stuffed Fish
    Rolls, 50

**W**
**Water chestnuts**
  Vegetables Oriental, 58

**Z**
**Zucchini**
  Garden Pasta Salad, 68
  Spicy Vegetable Cake, 91
  Tomato Vegetable Skillet,
    60
  Vegetable Lasagna, 49